History, People and Places in

THE LAKE DISTRICT

Church Beck

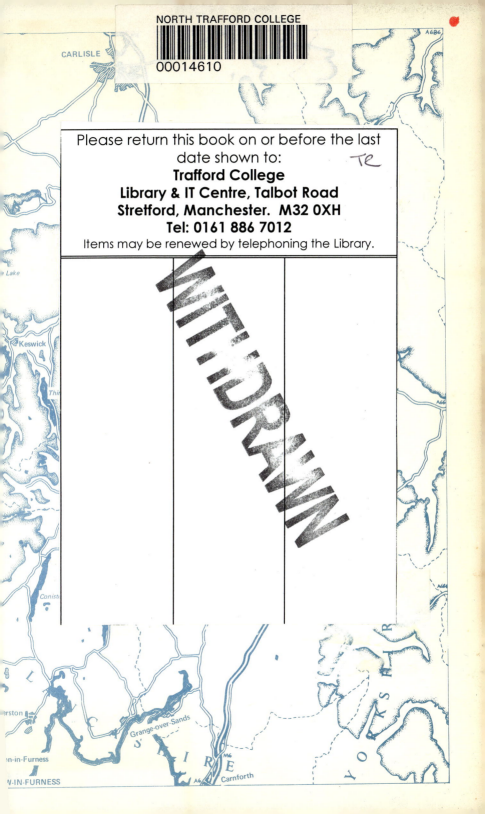

History, People and Places in

THE LAKE DISTRICT

Vera Burden

SPURBOOKS LIMITED

PUBLISHED BY
SPURBOOKS LTD
6 PARADE COURT
BOURNE END
BUCKINGHAMSHIRE

ISBN 0 904978 02 8

Designed and Produced by
Mechanick Exercises, London

Typesetting by Inforum, Portsmouth
Printed and bound in Great Britain
by Redwood Burn Limited,
Trowbridge and Esher

CONTENTS

ILLUSTRATIONS

ACKNOWLEDGMENTS

I would like to thank all those who have helped me during the writing of this book. I am especially grateful to Mr. K.S. Himsworth, of the National Park Special Planning Board, Mr. E. Wade of the Windermere Motor Boat Racing Club, the Librarian of the Freshwater Biological Association, Mr. B. Bilton of the Ruskin Museum, the Curator and Manager of Brantwood, the Manchester Waterworks and the National Trust, and, once again, the staff of the Barham Park Library. To Paddy, who undertook to read the manuscript, to Rose, who typed it, to Ben Hingston who helped with research, and to E.C.B. who, as always, generously gave encouragement and advice, I say thank you.

V.B.

USEFUL ADDRESSES IN THE LAKE DISTRICT NATIONAL PARK

NATIONAL PARK INFORMATION SERVICE
Bank House, High Street, Windermere, LA23 1AF

NATIONAL PARK OFFICE SPECIAL PLANNING BOARD
County Hall, Kendal, LA9 4RQ

CUMBRIA TOURIST BOARD
Ellerthwaite, Windermere

NATIONAL TRUST — LAKE DISTRICT OFFICE
Broadlands, Borrans Road, Ambleside, LA22 0EJ

FRESHWATER BIOLOGICAL ASSOCIATION
The Ferry House, Ambleside, Cumbria, LA22 0LP

Introduction

THE LURE OF THE LAKES

Two tents in a field within the shadow of Black Coombe heralded my introduction to the Lake District. We were a party of cousins, six of us, spending a camping holiday at Silecroft on the Cumbrian coast. On that first visit I was too young to join the excursions of my older cousins. They donned their climbing gear, gathered up packets of food, took a compass, and a copy of the indispensable Baddeley, and disappeared into the hinterland. Silecroft was to them a base camp to which they returned to replenish their stocks, sleep, and plan their next day out.

On a Sunday afternoon we would all explore the slopes of Black Coombe. I took no conscious heed of the view or the landscape. We scrambled, and ran, and laughed, revelling in the going up and the coming down and the drop scones we baked for tea when we returned to Farmer Brown's meadow. In the manner of young children, I envied the older ones as they talked enthusiastically of Gable, Wastwater, Coniston, Langdale, as of old and familiar friends. As the distinctive collection of Lakeland names became known to me, I was beguiled by their music, even before I had seen the splendours they signified.

That was simply the beginning.

In later years I also climbed the peaks, boated on the waters, and experienced the immeasurable pleasure of introducing others to this compact region of lake and fell, of solitary tarns, fast-moving rivers, crystal clear, and becks splashing dramatically over rock. A region where the capricious pattern of sun and shower, the magnificent sculpture of the mountains, the narrow, placid lakes compose an immutable yet ever-changing vista. Man, with all his creative genius, cannot compete with the timeless natural forces which have given us the English Lakes. Like a magnet, they have continued to draw me back again and again.

Now, of course, the Lake District is officially designated a National Park. Stretching from Caldbeck south to Cartmel, and from Gosforth east to Shap, the area is comparatively small, covering no more than 866 square miles in all. Also, instead of owing allegiance to three counties, Westmorland, Cumberland and Lancashire, it is, since April 1974, wholly contained by the reorganised county of Cumbria.

Whether it is called Cumbria, Lakeland, the Lake District National Park, or just, as the road signs depict, The Lakes, such is its appeal that, for the last two hundred years, a host of writers has been extolling its praise. To a writer that is a humbling thought. Yet, just as every new writer is eternally in the debt of those who have gone before, so every new volume is a further testimony to the lure of the Lakes.

When the idea of compiling my own book was taking shape, more often than not my thoughts turned to the lakes rather than upon the higher fells. So in the chapters which follow, whilst paying due homage to the grandeur of their setting, pride of place is given to the jewels of the Lake District, the lakes themselves.

1

WINDERMERE

It was the endearing writer Karel Capek who remarked that England was so proud of its lakes that it had a whole district allotted to them. In this unique region of fell and lake, which we do indeed call the Lake District, there are seventeen waters extensive enough to be called lakes.

Each one from Windermere, the largest, to Brotherswater, no longer than half a mile, has its own distinctive claim to beauty, grandeur, wildness, popularity or charm. Each has its own individuality; so the naturalist may be drawn to the shallow margins of Esthwaite, the yachtsman to the long island-less water of Bassenthwaite Lake, the Wordsworth pilgrims to Grasmere and Rydal, the seeker of the ever-decreasing wild and lonely places to Wastwater and the world to Windermere.

Windermere, a lake of the southern hills, is the mecca of those who delight in spending their leisure in, on or beside the water. Its sylvan surroundings, subdued, and less dramatic than the mountainous aspect of the more northern lakes, have long ensured it as a favourite holiday resort. Favourite viewpoints, Orrest Head, Queen Adelaide's Hill, Gummer's How ask to be climbed. Historic Belle Isle, wooded, romantic, reveals its unique Round House to all who stroll round Cockshot Point. The angler seeks a quiet bay or takes to his boat, and an occasional diver dons his protective garb at High Wray or Lakeside. Brockhole displays an ideal preview of the whole of the Lake District National Park, whilst at Fell Foot the National Trust has created a country park beside the lake shore. There are always the shore paths and the numerous islands to be explored, evoking memories of a colourful collection of Lakeland characters from Wordsworth to Beatrix Potter.

Propelled by sail, oar and engine, craft of all types frequent the superb inland waters. Launches, luxurious enough to be classed as mini-liners, call at Lakeside, Bowness and Waterhead. The ferry Drake ploughs its unvarying course from the Nab to Ferry House, the home of the freshwater biologists, and the Lake Warden from Parsonage Bay patrols the lake with a kindly and watchful eye.

Prior to the observant Mr. Watt watching his kettle and recognising the power of steam, oar propelled barges, hoisting a sail in fair winds, journeyed between Ambleside and Lakeside, carrying both passengers and cargo, taking up to three and a half hours to do so. The first wooden vessel to steam over Windermere was reputed to be the *Lady of the Lake*. She was owned by the Windermere Steam Yacht Company which started lake trips in the first half of the nineteenth century. The Wordsworth cult was flourishing, tourists had found the Lakes and the project was a distinct success.

It was not long before competition arrived in the form of an iron paddle steamer, *Fire Fly,* owned by the Iron Steam Boat

The Teal

Company. For a few years there was fierce rivalry between the two; sometimes a brass band playing on deck would be employed as an extra enticement. Initially the *Fire Fly* and the *Lady of the Lake* kept to different time-tables, and it must be admitted that the *Fire Fly* did not exactly further her own cause, being tempted to sail off on private cruises to the extreme annoyance of passengers awaiting her scheduled arrival. A further change, and both boats used the same time-table resulting in renewed bouts of indignation from all concerned as the boats arriving together at a landing tended to get in each other's way. Every means the owners could think of was used to gain custom, and the Steam Boat Company is said to have kept a man at Newby Bridge who rang a loud bell to attract passengers. In 1850 during the last two weeks of the season the *Lady of the Lake* would go round Windermere calling at any landing for the reduced fare of 6d. Not to be outdone, the *Fire Fly* immediately announced that no charge at all would be made!

Eventually, in 1858, the two companies merged, and three years later the *Lady* came to an unfortunate end when she ran ashore and had to be abandoned. Events moved rapidly, and when the railway from Newby Bridge was extended to Lakeside in 1872 the Steamboat Company was absorbed into the Furness Railway Company and a brand new fleet of vessels was launched — the *Swan, Teal, Tern, Swift* and *Cygnet*. These were the forerunners of British Rail's four Sealink cruisers, which now ply the lake in competition with the launches of private concerns. The Sealink cruisers alone carry around 500,000 passengers a year.

These were all boats for the tourist. But should you wander down to Bowness Pier during the winter months any boatman will point out to you, with some pride, a tried and trusted steel cargo boat, the *Raven*. This is her winter mooring, and in the summer she is to be discovered in honorable retirement behind Belle Isle. Built in 1871 as a Furness Railway steam engined barge and having been restored to her orginal condition, she is preserved as a showpiece. Believed to be the oldest registered steam vessel still in existence, she is certainly the oldest boat on Windermere. Vying with her in age is the graceful steam launch salvaged by George Patinson from the bottom of Ullswater. Remarkably, after resting on the lake bed for some eighty years, this vessel was raised to the surface with the cabin windows intact, and the short funnel still in position. Mr. Pattinson, a well-known local figure, is not alone in believing her to be the most elegant vessel on Windermere today.

Although not as yet on view, there are six other vessels of historic interest, each with a record of long service on Windermere. They are within the care of the Windermere Nautical Trust, which has plans for the construction of a dockyard in which they, and other unique craft, will be exhibited.

Then, of course, there is the ferry, Windermere and Derwentwater being the only two lakes with a ferry service. The origins of the Windermere ferry are lost in time, but in 1575 the Lords of Graythwaite Manor held the ferry rights and were paid an annual rent of 6s. 8d. Less than a hundred years later, in 1635, there came the tragic day when the ferry, transporting forty-seven people together with their horses and carriages returning in merry mood from Hawkshead Fair, 'either through the pressure and weight which surcharg'd her, or some violent and impetuous windes and waves that surpriz'd her', sank without a single survivor. So says the usual account, though the Grasmere parish register is said to mention 'one that escaped'.

It was honest, if hardly tactful of the Windermere guide who, when asked by the poet Thomas Gray while being ferried from the Nab to the Claife landing, if any lives had been lost from the ferry, related this story to him.

Gray was a man prone to exaggerated fears, to the amusement of more robust souls. When he visited the Lakes on his celebrated ten-day tour in 1769, he had come from the south to venture through an unknown region of awesome, precipitous mountains, and lakes, the dark depths of which had not as yet been fathomed. It was therefore hardly surprising that the ferryman's story alarmed him.

Gray is usually referred to as the first 'tourist'. This was due to the exquisite descriptions of the Lakes which he sent to his friend Dr. Wharton, who had at the last moment been unable to accompany him. But seventy years prior to Gray's visit Celia Fiennes had travelled on horseback through the Lake District during her 'great journey' across England. Without maps or guide books as we know them today she had arrived as if exploring a foreign country. She called the lakes 'standing waters', for they did not ebb and flow like the sea. They were quite unlike the rivers she had encountered, the Trent and the Thames. They were so deep, she commented, that the current of water that passed through them was 'scarce to be perceived'. Blessed with an observant eye, an adventurous spirit and an insatiable curiosity, the prim, matter-of-fact Miss Fiennes deserves more credit than she has received.

In the early days when the ferry was simply 'The Boat', one particular story which the ferrymen were wont to recount was the legend of the Claife Crier.

One night when the wind threatened and howled, the water of the lake was a black depth whipped into disarray by the gale, and the trepidation of those early travellers who saw nothing but menace in the surrounding fells would have been well understood. The ferryman at the Nab heard a call from the far unseen and wooded shore, 'Boat, Boat'. The familiar words rang out on a night when all sensible human beings were warmly within their own four walls. The ferryman responded to the call, as any good ferryman would, and rowed out across the uneasy water to collect his passenger. Others waited for him upon the shore, and when, after a considerable length of time had passed, the boat reappeared, those waiting saw it held no one but the ferryman. But the man who had rowed to Claife that night returned as if within the grasp of 'a devilish spirit'. Bereft of speech he was incapable of explaining the terrifying experience he had undergone. So when, not long afterwards he died, his story remained untold. Consequently that stretch of water across to Claife on the western shore was regarded as possessed by some evil which man could not resist. Again and again, after dark and when a tempest raged, the cry, 'Boat, Boat' would ring out across the lake. For years no ferryman would take his boat out after nightfall and the disturbing

17

Ferry Drake

heart-rending cry, went unanswered. Such was the effect upon the local people that at last it was they who appealed for help from:

> ' . . . *the good old monk of St. Mary's Holm*
> *With relics of Saints and beads from Rome,*
> *To row to the Nab on Halloween night*
> *And bury the Crier by morning's light.'*

After which, presumably, the ferryman slept soundly once again!

The first steam ferry arrived in 1869, and the present chain ferry which came into use in 1954 was converted to diesel in 1960. Designed to transport approximately ten cars, it pursues its endless journey from Ferry Nab on the eastern shore to Ferry House, conveying vehicles and pedestrians. So that we shall not forget that tourism and farming vie with each other as the primary industry of the Lakes, a glance at the schedule of tolls shows the collective charge for 'calves, pigs or sheep'.

The summer crossings are continuous from around seven in the morning till nine or ten at night, and at peak times motorists should be prepared for a queue involving a wait from fifteen minutes to, at its worst, two hours; sometimes it might be quicker to keep to the road after all.

One of the simple delights on sophisticated Windermere is the assortment of duck. During the winter when the water is more peaceful, the resident population is substantially increased by coot and other wintering wildfowl flying down from the frozen mountain tarns. Moreover, as dusk approaches the sky is alive with gulls winging over the fells to roost near Millerground Bay.

In summer both the duck and the more majestic swan, which swim on the ruffled waters of the lake, participate in the social life of Windermere, taking it for granted that picnics should be shared and that houseboat families include them in their catering. Parties of mallard entertain the ferry queues, causing moments of panic by claiming the middle of the road as their personal territory; and despite the numerous isles which provide them with good cover and shallower water in which to feed, they are constantly on the search for titbits. They are so intrinsic a part of the lake that when one of the larger lakeside hotels invested in a heated open-air swimming-pool the locals nodded wisely and remarked, 'The duck'll love it!' Sure enough they did, taking less time to discover the newly warmed pool than it did to persuade them to leave.

The serious human swimmers arrive in mid-summer to prepare themselves for the Long Distance Championships in August. The first person to swim the entire length of Windermere was a man named Foster from Oldham, who accomplished the feat in 1911, a year long remembered for its heatwave. Strangely enough, it was not swum again for twenty-two years, though since then all kinds of people, young and not-so-young, have responded to the challenge.

Swimming in Windermere, and in any of the lakes where it is permitted, should be undertaken with care and common sense. Lake water is notoriously cold; if, on a warm day, you

Parsonage Bay

pass your hand over the surface of the lake it is possible you may think this is an exaggeration. But only the upper layer of the water has absorbed the heat of the sun, and underneath it is still very cold. Windermere reaches a depth of 210 ft., and the bottom is deceptive, shelving very sharply in places. The local advice to swimmers is to use a recognised bathing place such as that at Millerground below Queen Adelaide's Hill; not to swim from a boat; not to over-estimate your own capabilities; and to take extra precautions against cramp. Also, on Windermere there is a lot of competition from the boating enthusiasts for water space!

Since the end of World War II the larger lakes, Windermere in particular, have been flooded by an influx of boating, sailing and water ski-ing devotees. All water sports have increased in popularity, and like much else, in availability.

There are flourishing local clubs such as The Royal Windermere Yacht Club, which claims to have the finest fleet of racing craft in the country, and rarely does a week-end pass without the racing of one class or another. The Windermere Motor Boat Racing Club, of which Donald Campbell was a member, has been in existence for fifty years. It is the senior powerboat racing club in the country, and is now fortunate in having Broadleys, a beautiful house on the eastern shore designed by Charles Voysey, as its headquarters. Water-speed records are more readily linked with Coniston and the Campbells, but it was on Windermere in 1930 that Henry Seagrave, piloting *Miss England II,* set up a new world record at 98.76 mph. Immediately, and without hesitation, he went out again to beat it, and crashed. His engineer was killed outright, and Seagrave died the next day.

Windermere's Motor Boat Club supported Seagrave, and has continued to assist in world record attempts that have taken place in Lakeland on Ullswater and Coniston with Campbell, and on Windermere with Norman Buckley and his *Miss Windermere.* The most recent record achieved by Buckley was with *Miss Windermere IV* when she broke the R5 world record at 114.187 mph. It was Norman Buckley and other friends of Campbell who formed the K7 Club, named after the number of Campbell's *Bluebird,* to promote record-breaking in the future.

After the majority of tourists have left, October is the month when Windermere sees the lovers of speed foregathering in force for the annual Grand Prix. This major event attracts international drivers to compete for the Duke of York Challenge Trophy, a not inconsiderable prize valued at £16,000. Following the excitement of the Grand Prix is a record week when boats of varying classes speed through the water in pursuit of new records.

It is, however, with the holidaymaker in mind that the South Lakeland District Council, owners of the bed of the lake, have published a *Chart of Lake Windermere.* The rule of the road is, of course, that boats under power give way to boats under sail. With the advent of water ski-ing and increase in powerboats, it has become necessary to introduce speed limits of 10 mph on the extreme northern and southern areas of the lake, together with an area in Bowness Bay. The Council's lucid *Chart*, purchased at very little cost, contains all that should be known concerning the speed restrictions, rocks, shallow water, launching, mooring, piers and the rules it is incumbent on all users of the lake to keep for safety and good conduct in or on the water.

When water ski-ing was first introduced into the Lake District it was the subject of much criticism. Novel, and with a tremendous appeal to those who are exhilarated by the adventure of speed, it is a pastime which, from its birth in the States, quickly spread around the world. Unfortunately, the exhilaration of the participants and the interest of the spectators—for it is arresting to watch—is not always shared by others who may be enjoying the water in their own calmer fashion, notably fishermen, swimmers and navigators of light craft. Over the years a steady flow of protest has reached the ears of the various authorities controlling the use of the lakes.

It is, therefore, welcome news that the Special Planning Board, using for the first time the powers vested in them under the Countryside Act of 1968, have issued bye-laws concerning the control of boats on twenty of the lakes and tarns. They prohibit the use of any vessel propelled by an internal combustion engine, including flying boats and aircraft! The major lakes included in this 'full score for peace and quiet' are Bassenthwaite Lake, Buttermere, Crummock, Esthwaite, Grasmere, Loweswater, Rydal and Wastwater.

The *Low Wood Hotel,* scene of Wordsworth's and his fellow protesters' bid to stop the railway being extended to Windermere, and of Ruskin's boyhood visit, is now a recognised meeting place for skiers.

The main concern is to maintain a safe and equable water for the enjoyment of all. Happily, the Lake Police and the Wardens who patrol the lake during the season are always on the alert for anyone who, through ignorance or lack of consideration, may be likely to put themselves or others at risk. 'We like to get there before the accident happens,' one of the Lake Policemen told me. They are to be congratulated on the success of their vigilance for very few accidents do occur on Windermere.

One sport which modern Windermere rarely sees is ice skating. But Windermere of two hundred years ago is recalled as a place where the lake was so solidly frozen that the regular wrestling contests took place on the ice, with the attendant extravagance of a fire to roast an ox. In 1895 a sheet of ice stretched from shore to shore for six whole weeks. Skaters of every size and shape sped over the frozen surface to the music of the hurdy-gurdy man, and of a brass band bravely risking frozen fingers. Then the ice was eighteen inches thick, and bore the weight of thousands of people. The most memorable freeze of this century was in 1928 when cars were driven on to the ice, and the most recent, during the severe winter of 1962/63, which was one of the coldest on record.

First the railway, then the car, and now the speed of the M6 have all contributed to the accessibility of the Lake District. Of those who come just for the day, or an afternoon's excursion from the neighbouring northern towns, the majority go no further than Windermere. The stranger who arrives to discover Bowness on the margin of the lake, whilst the village of Windermere to the north-east collects itself about the station, may reasonably ask how this came to be. Before the railway there was no village of Windermere, and the railway authorities, unable to build their station any nearer to the lake, had to be content with establishing it beside the handful of houses known as Birthwaite. But who, they asked themselves, would ever wish to take a train to Birthwaite? thus with astute business acumen they re-named it Windermere. Now, to bring us up-to-date, it has, with Bowness, a population of over 8,000, but the station, alas, has lost its through trains and travellers from the south must change at Oxenholme.

At the height of the season, a season which annually seems to incorporate an extra week or two—March to the end of October is scarcely an exaggeration—sightseers throng the

Patrol Boat and Swans, Windermere

winding streets of Bowness. Having selected their cards, bought their ice-creams or sipped their coffee and discussed the gifts to take back home, they wander down to the pier, as in any seaside resort. And for some the height of enjoyment seems to be just to sit and watch the skill and antics of others who mess about in boats.

On this eastern shore hotels, houses, gardens, boatsheds, piers, all intermingle. In the eighteenth and nineteenth centuries wealthy people, including many who grew rich in the Lancashire industrial towns, bought land beside Windermere, built lavish mansions, and planned extensive gardens. Much of the land is still privately owned and access to the shore is limited. If the road running along the eastern side does not, therefore, present a very welcoming aspect, let it be no matter for regret, for there are nearly 1,000 square miles of the Lake District to be explored. Anyway, nothing is static, properties do change hands and in very recent years at least two of the estates on Windermere's shore have opened their gates to us all.

Wordsworth was the first to have a vision of the Lake District as a national property 'in which every man has a right and interest who has an eye to perceive and a heart to enjoy'. Moves towards making this a reality began with the foundation of the National Trust, but it was not until 1951 that the Lake District was officially designated as a National Park. Since 1969 the Lake District National Park has had its own centre at Brockhole, about half way between Windermere and Ambleside on the A591. It is the first centre of its kind in the country and as a prelude to the Lakeland theme it is a distinct success.

Formerly the home of a Manchester businessman, Brockhole, using varied modern display techniques, presents an audio-visual story of the Lake District covering every aspect from its geological formation to the present day. From time to time one of the staff strolls among the visitors to announce that a short talk or film is about to begin. This welcoming informality combined with first-class organisation make it an ideal outing, especially for newcomers to the Lakes. Highly informative, it has ample literature and leaflets, some of them free, covering climbing, sailing, fishing, lake trips and every conceivable leisure activity. There are maps, models and books, a quiet room, and an attractive pinewood restaurant facing the meticulously tended formal gardens.

At the beginning of the eighteenth century, Fell Foot at the

25

Brockhole

southern end of the lake facing Lakeside, was the small estate of a family named Robinson, and in 1774 it passed to Jeremiah Dixon of Leeds. Dixon's wife was the daughter of John Smeaton who designed the Eddystone Lighthouse and often stayed at Fell Foot. Smeaton is, in fact, remembered more vividly in Ulverston where a memorial to him can be seen on Hoad Hill.

In 1859 Fell Foot came into the ownership of Colonel Ridehalgh, a founder of the Royal Windermere Yacht Club and a man of initiative who transformed his strip of the foreshore. He constructed a miniature dockyard for his various boats, and also owned a pack of hounds which he transported by boat, often using the western shore jetty at Wray Castle as a landing. He added an original touch to Fell Foot by generating

Lakeside from Fell Foot

his own coal gas, and a line of gas lamps lit the lake edge. He planted ornamental trees as was the custom of his time, and rhododendrons which have since rampaged beyond their allotted boundary.

When the Colonel died Fell Foot was sold to Oswald W. E. Hedley who had grand ideas for erecting a new house. The original house was demolished in 1906, but new building did not progress beyond the laying of the foundations, for on the death of his first wife Hedley moved to Calgarth Hall (now an Outdoor Pursuits Centre). Fell Foot was abandoned till 1948 when it passed to the Trust.

After twenty-one years of being leased as a caravan camp site, Fell Foot has been developed into an 18 acre Country Park. The foundations of the house the Hedleys never built

27

serve as a discreet car park for those who wish to spend a semi-private day beside Windermere. The longest of the dry boat-houses, glorified by a portcullis and a minstrel's gallery, has been converted into a cafe, flying the green Trust flag. The South Windermere Sailing Club is established alongside, there is a launching ramp for craft other than powerboats, and Fell Foot is a regular call on the lake launches' schedule. Control of traffic is one of the National Park's most pressing problems. If Fell Foot diverts only a fraction from the highways I, for one, give it my blessing.

About four miles north of Fell Foot is Storrs Temple, the octagonal folly built by Sir John Legard Storrs. Initially known as The Temple of Heroes, it honoured Admirals Howe, Nelson and Duncan. Connected to the shore by a stone causeway it is preserved as an interesting feature of the landscape and, like most follies, regarded with affection. Regard it from the water, or from nearby Beech Hill, is all we may do, as it has been thought wiser not to allow public access.

Here the celebrated group including Scott, Canning and Wordsworth watched the Regatta organised by Professor Wilson in honour of Scott's fifty-fourth birthday. A stream of gaily decorated boats moved in procession up the lake. The sun shone, there were bright dresses, cannons were fired, and above the rapid splashings of innumerable oars was heard the sound of two bands playing simultaneously, with great gusto, but rendering different tunes.

Wilson, the 'Christopher North' of Blackwoods Magazine, combined an intense love for the Lake country with an enormous physical capacity for taking in all the open air recreations offered by the challenge of both mountain and water. As a young poet in Oxford he wrote to Wordsworth, whom he knew only by name, a letter of 'effusive admiration' which led to friendship. In 1807 he arrived in the Lakes, met and married Jane Penney, a Lancashire girl living in Ambleside, and they set up home at Elleray, near Orrest Head.

Wilson, wealthy and exuberant, breezed into the coterie of the Lake Poets, winning the hearts of all he met by his sheer joy in living. 'He made others happy by being so intensely happy himself,' applauded his contemporary, Harriet Martineau. After settling at Elleray he established a fleet of vessels on Windermere. No expense was spared; skilled workmen from Whitehaven were brought to Bowness to build the boats. This vigorous extravagance led to Canning dubbing Wilson 'The High Admiral of the Lakes'.

Wilson had arrived rich and trouble-free, but on losing his wealth overnight due to an uncle's mishandling, was forced to return to Edinburgh where he furthered his literary career with Blackwoods. Elleray was retained, but after his beloved Jane died the memories were too poignant and his visits from Edinburgh ceased. Eventually the house was demolished, but its name lives on. We may still contemplate, as the Wilsons did, the superb view from Orrest Head, with the southern and central reaches of the lake spreading out to the sylvan heights of Claife.

Professor Wilson was one of many, before and since, to extol the charm of Troutbeck. Not the rather bleak Troutbeck beyond Ullswater, but the wooded and picturesque Troutbeck which hurries its sparkling stream through the deep valley into Windermere.

Here lived the Troutbeck Giant, Thomas Hogarth, uncle of William Hogarth the painter, and the Brownes. The Brownes were a Westmorland family of yeoman farmers, or 'statesmen', who occupied the house known as Townend from 1623 until 1944. Without doubt they had been established in Troutbeck from an even earlier time. From 1525 onwards each generation produced a George Browne of Townend, until the last direct line was survived by three daughters, Lucy, Clara and Katharine, none of whom married, and the house passed into the ownership of the Trust.

The seven circular chimneys, the slate roof and rough cast walls are all characteristic of Westmorland, the county to which Troutbeck formerly belonged. The oldest part of the building is the centre; the wings at either side were added later. The last George Browne immersed himself in local history, and was far-sighted enough to realise the value of preserving the domestic contents of Townend for their future historical

Townend, Troutbeck

interest. So the out-dated metal cheese press, milk churns, flat iron for ruffs, rushlight holders, mangle, wooden washing machine with a hefty handle to be turned, and other utensils which might have been discarded, are intact. The Brownes had a flair for woodwork and joinery, carving for themselves oak furniture—including beds, chairs, chests—engraved with dates and initials. Downstairs an array of cupboards, drawers, and even a long-cased clock are grouped along the walls to form an unexpected 'fitted' kitchen of much-used and highly polished oak.

Townend is an amiable, individual house offering a unique glimpse into the life of a Lakeland family, with no claim to national fame, but who were typical yeoman farmers, hardy as the sheep they bred, wresting their living from the land and passinr down their knowledge and skills from one generation to the next.

2

WINDERMERE—WEST TO ESTHWAITE

Waterhead, where Windermere receives two rivers beloved by
the poets and with names so easily confused—the Rothay and
the Brathay—is the landing stage for the ancient market town
of Ambleside. At the foot of the 'Struggle' up to the Kirkstone
pass, enclosed by the sheltering mountains, Loughrigg and
Wansfell, with Nab Scar, Fairfield and High Pike, to the
north, it vies with Keswick as the ideal centre for fell walkers
and sightseers. Like all Lakeland towns it wears a permanent
holiday air; that is, except for the lorries which will disrupt its
daily life for as long as they have no alternative route to take.
Ambleside, whether we arrive by boat, car, coach or on foot, is
there to feed and shelter us, sell us boots, life-jackets, anoraks,
sailing caps, fishing tackle, or just sandwiches, and direct us
towards fresh lakes and mountains new.

But its own long history and recollections of the Lake poets,
of Dr. Arnold, of Fox How, Hartley Coleridge and his friend,
Owen Lloyd, composer of the Rushbearing hymn, still sung
on the occasion of the traditional July ceremony, of Rev.
R.W. Faber, a much-loved minor poet, and the host of eminent Victorian personalities who journeyed to The Knoll to
visit Miss Martineau, invite us to linger awhile.

There is the up-dated *Salutation Hotel* reviving memories
of the boy Ruskin whom it pleased, and Gray whom it did not.
Had we been able to look into its largest room one November
evening in 1850, we would have beheld a gathering of people,
including Wordsworth's son-in-law, Edward Quillinan and
Harriet Martineau, watching the most modern entertainment

31

of the day, 'An Exhibition of Dissolving Views and Crom-tropes'.

And it is behind the *Salutation* that the well-worn path climbs through an open glade, no less beautiful for being popular, to discover the Stock Ghyll Force cascading over the rock of Wansfell in a 76 ft. drop. Once, as it raced on down, the water helped to operate a bobbin mill, on a site now marked by holiday flats. In the town everyone is attracted to the Old Bridge House, now believed to have been a garden house in the grounds of Ambleside Hall, though there used to be people in Ambleside who would tell you this diminutive dwelling served as a waiting-room for coaches. The travellers sat upstairs, whilst their servants waited downstairs with the luggage. Whatever its original purpose, the National Trust have now put it to good use as an Information Centre.

As Wordsworth, in his lifetime, attracted visitor after visitor to Grasmere, so did Miss Martineau to Ambleside.

Norfolk-born Harriet Martineau, whose deafness from childhood necessitated the use of an ear-trumpet, was, through her outspoken articles on the social and political topics of the day, a distinguished name in contemporary literary circles. In middle life she retired from the world with a chronic illness. After reclining ' on a sofa ' for six years, a sudden interest in mesmerism had a therapeutic effect. Having recovered her health she decided to settle in the Lakes.

Wordsworth, now seventy-six, welcomed her, and on learning that she had purchased two fields in Ambleside at an auction, complimented her on her choice of site. With typical prudence it was not the charm of the Lakeland he bore in mind, but that the property would double in value in ten years time.

So in 1855 she established her home at The Knoll and took up the Lakes with gusto. Through her efforts a group of new cottages was built to relieve overcrowding. When asked to write a *Guide to the Lakes,* she set about it with her usual energy, exploring the whole district exhaustively one summer. Apart from writing, the undertaking which gave her most delight was lecturing to the nearby villages. She was renowned

Stock Ghyll Force

for her six or seven mile walks before breakfast, prior to which she took a cold bath, the bath being in a little barn some thirty yards or so away from the house. According to town gossip, the redoubtable Miss Martineau walked from house to barn in the nude.

Most of the leading notables of the day were known to her. George Eliot, Emerson and Darwin numbered among those who travelled to Ambleside to visit her; Charlotte Bronte drove to The Knoll when staying with the Shuttleworths at Briery Close, where she first met her biographer-to-be, Elizabeth Gaskell. ' Miss Martineau I relish inexpressibly — all she does is well done from the writing of a history down to the quietest female occupation ', wrote Charlotte after that first visit. Miss Martineau was, however, known for her forthright manner, and when later her criticism of *Villette* upset Charlotte they became estranged.

Neither did Miss Martineau always agree with her neighbour, Wordsworth. He opposed the coming of the railway, whereas she believed the introduction of outsiders into the Lakes was needed, and encouraged it. She could hardly do otherwise, she was an ' off-comer ' herself. Nevertheless, when curious tourists descended upon The Knoll, peered into her windows, plucked her flowers and generally treated her as one of Ambleside's attractions, it proved more than she could bear, and she chose to go away for the busiest months of the year. This was one of the penalties of fame.

When Mrs. Wordsworth asked Harriet to visit them in the evenings, thinking she would be company for the elderly poet, the invitation was refused. Certainly, to have driven to Rydal Mount and back at the end of the day would have been quite an undertaking, but Harriet's refusal was more honestly based on the fact that William, she knew, removed his teeth in the evening and mumbled so that she would not have heard a word he said!

The Knoll, just off the Rydal road, where Harriet Martineau lived until her death in 1876, is now privately occupied and memories of its first remarkable occupant grow fainter over the years.

Old Bridge House, Ambleside

On the banks of the Brathay where, taking the Rothay and the Stock Beck with it, the river is about to disappear into the lake, is Borrans Field. Strategically positioned at the head of Windermere it was on this site that, nearly 2,000 years ago the Romans built Galava Fort. Even the Romans made the odd constructional mistake, it seems, for their first effort was flooded when the river overflowed its banks. Now the main difference of Borrans Field from any other green sward is that it commands an outstanding view of the lake. To gain a more realistic image of Galava it is best to return to Brockhole, which now harbours the fragments of Roman pottery and other relics excavated by R.G. Collingwood.

Moving west out of Ambleside we quickly arrive at Clappersgate, which once served as a port for Langdale slate transferred by barges and sent down Windermere. Before Cumbria widened its arms to include the whole of the Lake District, crossing the bridge at Clappersgate meant moving from Westmorland into Lancashire. The nearby Outward Bound Centre occupies Brathay Hall, once the home of John Harden, the nineteenth-century water colour artist, whilst Old Brathay has its associations with Charles Lloyd, friend to all the Lake Poets.

With one road following a delightful route through Outgate to Hawkshead, and the other accommodating motorists to Langdale and Coniston, this junction is too busy a spot for the pedestrian, except for turning aside to White Craggs.

During the early part of the twentieth century, C.E. Hough and his family, all keen amateur gardeners, exercised themselves in an original type of excavation.

Denuding a hillside below Loughrigg of its covering of coppice wood, they revealed a rockscape of unexpected grandeur. Into the crevices left by the uprooted timber they planted alpines, flowering shrubs, heathers, azaleas of infinite variety collected from all over the world. Through the untiring and loving efforts of the Hough family there emerged White Craggs, a natural rock garden of quite superlative beauty, to which, since 1919, the public have always been welcome. At the top of the winding path are seats from which to look down

Claife Shore

upon the massed array of blossom, and out over Windermere. No charge is, or has ever been made for the joy this lake rock garden gives; gratitude may be expressed by contributing to the collecting box for charity.

The western shore of Windermere is undomesticated, wilder and far more accessible than its eastern counterpart. Even during the annual August fever, a short stroll away from the regular haunts may discover a retreat for those who prefer less populous regions.

Below Claife, where March and April display a golden burst of daffodil, the water laps a beach sprinkled with silver birch, and venerable oak have visible roots hardly distinguishable from the ever-present rock. For those who like to have their walks waymarked there is a six-mile excursion from the Ferry to Hawkshead, opened by the Duke of Edinburgh in 1966. Similarly, Harrowslack, where the Trust, caretaker of a fair proportion of this shore, operates a small saw-mill, is the land-mark for nature trails leading up into the Claife woods, and along the shore. Basically educational, nature trails have become widespread and immensely popular. It is good to stand, as the trail leaflet suggests, upon Coatlap Point, to pause and look around. Immediately south are Maiden Holme and Crow Holme, two of the rocky hummocks smoothed by the ice, which we know as islands. In the fore-ground the elongated finger of Belle Isle curves away towards the head of the lake.

The first known occupiers of Belle Isle's 38 acres were the De Lindesays in the fourteenth century, when it was known as Long or Great Holme. Later it was owned by the Phillipsons, manorial owners of Windermere, who as staunch Royalists, were besieged on the island for eight months during the Civil War. In 1774 we find it belonging to a Mr. English, who employed John Plaw to design a unique cylindrical house with a dome and a portico; the first mansion in the Lake District built specifically as a picturesque house in a picturesque set-ting. But not long after it was completed Mr. English chose to sell his island home to the Curwens. Isabella Curwen was the wealthy daughter of a Workington man who amassed a for-tune from the northern coalfields. She married John Chris-tian, a Manxman, who added her name to his own and was henceforth known as John Christian Curwen. Although Pevsner tends to the belief that it is the Round House which makes the isle *belle*, Isabella Curwen is more generally accepted as the inspiration of its present name.

Today, it is Windermere's only inhabited isle and boats sail across from the jetty near Cockshot Point conveying passeng-ers to relax in the fields, rose gardens and rhododendron walk.

One of the first picturesque descriptions of the Lakes is a seventeenth-century reference by Richard Braithwaite to 'the curiously shaded, beauteously tufted islands of Windermere'. Mainly secretive in appearance when viewed from the shore, and even allowing for the surge of nautical life enveloping them for most months of the year, they are still touched by romance. Ladyholme, just south of Rayrigg Wyke, was a sacred isle with a chantry chapel. There is no trace of it today, though monks lived here in seclusion until 1549. Silverholme has its legend of buried treasure, and Lilies of the Valley requires no explanation. Reaction to the name Ramp Holme (Rampsholme belongs to Derwentwater) may not be so immediate, but it too owes its name to the flowers of wild garlic, otherwise ramsons, which flourished here.

There being seventeen isles altogether, I will not pause to account for them all, but Hen Holme is 'water-hen island', a 'water-hen' being the more accurate name for moorhen; and a bygone belief that the Devil dropped stones from his apron, or skirt, gave rise to Skirtful Crags, a well-marked danger point below Gummers How.

These islands of Windermere are best loved for the childhood memories they evoke. For the schoolboy Wordsworth:

'It was the pastime of our afternoons
To beat along the plain of Windermere
With rival oars, and the selected bourne
Was now an Island musical with birds
That sang for ever; now a Sister Isle
Beneath the oak's umbrageous covert sown
With lilies of the valley, like a field.'

In our time the vivid recollection of his own youthful adventures on Windermere and Coniston inspired Arthur Ransome in the creation of his lively stories for children. Similarly, in the surroundings of Wray Castle, a nineteenth-century Gothic-style extravagance above Watbarrow Point, another child, Beatrix Potter, became familiar with the Lake country. We too, now have the opportunity to explore Wray Castle's grounds and woodland sloping irresistibly down to Windermere. A new generation of children wearing their Boy Scout uniform set up camp in a part of its 64 acres. To them, to the young Beatrix, to innumerable children, past and present, the Lake District is a holiday world glorified by the freedom to splash in the gushing becks, scramble over the lower fells, to fish, to scan the shallows for minnows and sticklebacks, and to observe the wild life a town-dweller rarely sees.

The thousands of printed words devoted to Beatrix Potter since her death in 1943, and the film of her Tales, has made Hill Top, the farmhouse in Sawrey which she left to the Trust, so fashionable a venue, that to write of her might seem superfluous; following in the footsteps of *Jemima Puddleduck*, and other familiar characters, 64,000 people walked up the long garden path of Hill Top in one year. Nevertheless, to omit her is impossible. Let us though, concentrate on her private life as Mrs. Heelis, wife of a country solicitor.

After her marriage the creative period of her life drew to a sudden close, but Hill Top, purchased when she was thirty-nine, was so essential a part of her that when she moved to Castle Cottage, a mere meadow's breadth away, she felt the need to retain it exactly as it stood—little changed from the way it is today. The village of Sawrey, situated above Esthwaite, is surrounded by subdued Lakeland scenery. The neighbouring hills above Esthwaite and Windermere have neither the challenge nor the dramatic impact of the northern peaks. This is pastoral farming land where the talk was of branding, dipping, shearing and the price of wool. As a child Beatrix studied the natural life of the Lake District with a keen eye and an eager mind, and with equal absorption Mrs. Heelis assimilated the practices and principles of sheep farming. When Troutbeck Park, an isolated and lonely farm, came on the market she bought it together with a stock of several hundred mountain sheep, and on this farm she would listen and learn, eventually becoming a highly respected authority on the local Herdwicks; a considerable achievement for an 'off-comer'. Mrs. Heelis had, as she was proud to aver, merely returned to the land of her north country ancestors.

In her own solid, brusque and totally unsentimental fashion, Mrs. Heelis cared passionately about the Lakes not being exploited. Gradually she purchased land and a number of farms, and after her death a total of 4,000 acres, including Tarn Hows and the Monk Coniston estate, represented her contribution towards the National Trust's preservation of the landscape she loved. The Trust's policy, in which she fervently believed, is to maintain the active life of all its Lake District

Hill Top, Near Sawrey

farms, and it now has a larger stock of Herdwicks than any other landowner.

Mrs. Heelis continued the battle against all scarring of the countryside which her friend, Canon Rawnsley, whom she first met as Vicar of Wray, had begun. Dressed for the weather, in the local clogs, with numerous shawls and heavy tweeds clothing her comfortable figure, she would personally remove litter discarded by less caring beings from the hill or way-side. Conversation with the people of Sawrey who knew her, suggests that she took a pride in her own non-conformity, that the formidable Mrs. Heelis was not always liked, and there were those with whom she quarrelled. But in all probability she has given more lasting pleasure, by her double legacy to children and their parents, than any other writer of children's books. *Peter Rabbit* is the only book of my own very early years of which I can actually remember turning over the pages. Years later, I was enchanted to discover that it was Beatrix Potter herself, for so long a disembodied name, who had insisted that her books should be small enough for a child's hands.

Long after it had forsaken its role as a holiday home for wealthy Victorian families, Wray Castle witnessed the foundation of the Freshwater Biological Association under the directorship of Dr. W.H. Pearsall, who had been studying the lakes since before World War I, travelling everywhere by cycle and rowing over the lakes. It is consistent with its modest financial backing of subscriptions amounting to £575, and an equivalent grant from the Government, that in those initial days the F.B.A. occupied only three rooms of the Castle. The rest of the building was in use as a Youth Hostel, and a wire fence ran down the middle of the staircase to divide hostellers from biologists. Since 1950 the biologists have established themselves in the modernised and extended site of Ferry House, and Wray Castle acts as a training school for the Merchant Navy.

Ferry House, on the Claife shore, replaced the *Old Ferry Inn* known to all the eminent Lake District characters. There are those who regret it is no longer a hostelry. While appreciating the sigh of nostalgia for its passing, were it still an inn it would only add to the amount of traffic already using the

Wray Castle

limited approach to the ferry landing whereas, as it is, the holidaymaker is not tempted to dally by the strictly scientific headquarters of the freshwater biologists, except possibly on their occasional 'open day'. However, as he follows the winding road to Esthwaite and Hawkshead, or turns south to Cunsey and across the Furness Fells, he might speculate on the work of these dedicated researchers.

In the early days one biologist moored his boat in the middle of Windermere, and stayed there for twenty-four hours. His purpose was to measure periodically the temperature of the water at different depths. A rowing boat is still the *modus operandi*, but equipped with assorted, less tedious instruments for measuring temperatures, or collecting water samples, and a winch to assist in lowering them to the required depth. We came upon a party of visiting students from Edinburgh one morning setting out with a lengthy pole-like apparatus designed to obtain samples of deposit from the lake bed for analysis. This ingenious instrument enabled samples to be extracted from a depth of up to 250 ft.

Unless you happen to be a fisherman, or a biologist, the life below the surface of these inland waters being out of sight may feasibly be also out of mind. But when a marked variance occurs in the underwater pattern then the biologists of Ferry House ponder more deeply upon their laboratory findings.

This caused the story of the Windermere perch which gained renown during World War II.

Until net fishing ceased entirely at the beginning of this century Windermere had been managed for its char fishing, which had long been a profitable Lakes industry. On the other hand visitors arriving for a week or two's quiet sport were more likely to go perch fishing. It was, prior to the invention of speedboats, considered one of Windermere's most important tourist attractions.

About the end of the 1920s the talk was of the vast numbers of perch in Windermere. In August 1927 one man caught 137 in one evening. Catches were large, the perch were exceedingly small. The tales of experienced anglers who recalled more rewarding catches of previous years were decidedly not all tall

Ferry House

stories. At the same time there were, it was thought, less of the much-valued char and trout, with which the perch competed for food. It seemed probable that the decline would continue as long as the massive perch population flourished.

Ferry House, encouraged by the anglers, believed if the numbers were reduced the perch would grow to a larger size, as might also the char and trout. The idea was sound, though how to set about it posed a problem.

As it turned out the outbreak of war hastened the experiment out of the laboratory and into the lake.

With the onset of hostilities in 1939 the country was forced to explore all possibilities of food production, and here was Lake Windermere awash with edible, though tiny, perch. In

1941 the number of adult perch in the lake was estimated at 5 million. Many of the perch making up this staggering figure weighed no more than one ounce, and who was inspired to suggest canning them I do not know, but that, need it be said, is what happened.

The idea, when put into practice, resulted in a concerted local effort characteristic of the time.

A series of specially devised traps, resembling lobster pots, with an entrance hole only three inches wide — to exclude other species — successfully removed large numbers of perch from the lake. A Leeds firm canned them like sardines, and 'Perchines' took their place upon the war-time grocer's shelf.

The trapping was a seasonal and hectic affair, lasting about six weeks from late April to early June. Once the canning began practically every local resident who owned a rowing boat, and many who did not, offered assistance and spent their evening in emptying the traps and delivering the catch to a fixed landing point, from whence a lorry transported the fish to Leeds. In the first year of this large-scale enterprise 380 traps caught one million perch weighing 25 tons! Windermere had returned briefly to commercial fishing.

The result of the long-term experiment has been that, although removal of perch has now ceased, their numbers have not recovered, and larger perch are now being caught. Ferry House has pleased the anglers, and in further efforts to improve the fishery, a percentage of pike has been removed from the lake, thus increasing the survival of adult char. Every now and again an unsuspecting fisherman may reel in his line to discover he has hooked a tagged perch, pike or whatever species is currently under F.B.A. observation. If he returns it to Ferry House he will probably find his co-operation is rewarded.

Lake Windermere is now so busy a water that anglers frequently take to a boat when the solitude which their sport requires grows more difficult to locate. Perch fishermen favour the southern narrower regions of the lake where the Leven takes over. Those who indulge in the specialised sport of trolling for char tend to maintain an air of mystery about

Newby Bridge

their technique. Char, lurking in the depths, need to be tempted with a shiny lure, and who is to say whether tales of wedding rings beaten down, or gold sovereigns passed from father to son for this purpose, are wholly exaggerated?

Had we been making our tour of Windermere a century ago it might well have begun from Lakeside. For Lakeside, Windermere's southern landing stage, was a focal point of nineteenth-century tourism. Following the extension of the Furness Railway to Lakeside in 1869, it was used by holidaymakers from Blackpool and other northern towns, who found it an ideal gateway to the Lakes. On alighting from the train they could immediately embark on the *Swan* to take them to Waterhead or Bowness.

Wealthy shipbuilders came to live in lakeside homes and used the line to Barrow-in-Furness. At one time Belsfield at Bowness, now the *Belsfield Hotel,* was the home of Schneider

of Vickers. His land ran down to the lake shore, and a colourful story tells that each day he walked down to the pier, followed by his butler with breakfast on a silver tray, to board his
private launch. There, presumably, he indulged in a leisurely
breakfast, and on arrival at Lakeside simply stepped off his
boat into his private train, which delivered him more or less to
his office door in Barrow.

Rather surprisingly Lakeside Station did not close till 1965.
For a few years the gates were closed, the rails were silent and
only the weeds and grass prospered. Then, due to the energy of
a dedicated group imbued with nostalgia for the Steam Age,
3½ miles of the track were re-opened. The Lakeside and
Haverthwaite Railway, confined to a May to September service, has also, by a judicious arrangement with the Cruisers'
time-table, revived Windermere's tradition of railboat excursions, the trains being scheduled to connect with either a private, or a Sealink cruiser.

The seasonal bustle at Lakeside, well viewed from the
quieter banks of Fell Foot over the water, marks it as a honeypot area. It claims to have the best equipped car park in Britain, which means that having parked your vehicle, and paid
the required parking fee, you may board the *Swift* or one of
her sister ships, and indulge in a cruise round the lake. A cruise
is an ideal way of delighting in every lovely prospect of Windermere in just two and a half hours. Should you not have visited
the restaurant on the voyage, then a cafeteria dedicated to the
Norsemen awaits your return, and anything from a deck chair
to fishing tackle may be hired nearby. The renaissance of the
steam engines has added the final flourish.

Travelling around the Lakes, more usually beside the southern lakes and streams, it is not uncommon to come across the
relics of an abandoned bobbin mill. Bobbin mills employed
hundreds of men and children of the Lake District during the
last century. To the few they brought riches. Not far from
Lakeside, at Stott Park on the Hawkshead road, the last survivor of the bobbin mills finally closed its doors in 1970.

The deserted buildings of Coward's Mill hold the story of an
industry which lasted for less than a century. Ash, birch, wil-

Lakeside

low, and other slender-branched trees, supplied the wood, and water-power was at hand; the bobbins, simply turned, were easily despatched to the Lancashire cotton factories. Labour was the only shortage, and men were encouraged to bring their young sons into the trade. Nowadays, reconciliation of the Lakeland image with the Victorian exploitation of child labour hardly seems possible. Yet in the first years of the bobbin mills, boys worked long hours, had little fresh air and were assailed by persistent dust. Eventually conditions improved, but not before many children, unable to exercise their young limbs properly, had become victims of tuberculosis and anaemia.

A few years after its closure we paid a visit to Stott Park. Lengths of coppice wood were still stacked in one of the drying sheds. In these sheds, best described as roofs on stilts, the wood, felled after about fourteen years, remained for a further eighteen months or so until it was dry enough for use. A scattering of bobbin-sized sections lay in the yard where nettles and cow parsley now met no opposition. Round at the back by the stream we saw evidence of the old water wheel. Most haunting of all was the deserted workshop, a typical two-storey building with a long row of windows below which the lathes were set, and the out-dated machines festooned with cobwebs. Every surface held its small pile of sawdust. Tools, odd tins and scraps of rag lay about as if one night the men had left as usual, intending to return, but fate had stepped in and stopped them. By now a decision may have settled the destination of these remnants of a pre-plastic age which, like the iron-smelting and charcoal burning, put the Lakeland waters to industrial use. Talk has hovered over the idea of a museum which would always, one of its proponents suggested, keep our knowledge of the past clear, and give us somewhere to go if it rains!

One of the numerous sparkling streams between Windermere and Coniston, beside which iron was once made 'in the bloomery way', is the Cunsey Beck, the link between Windermere and Esthwaite. Slipping into existence under Ees Bridge it is the escape for Esthwaite's surplus water, carrying it into Windermere opposite Lingholme.

50

Bobbin Mill, Stott Park

Esthwaite is small, just 1½ miles long and half a mile wide. It lies, like Windermere, in pastoral landscape. The prospect across the low fells to the pikes of Langdale is verdant and unpretentious. The underlying rock of Bannisdale slates, hard, yet not as hard as the northern volcanic series, responded more readily to the moulding of the ice sheets and gave birth to this gentle vista of rounded contours and smoothly curving wooded hills.

Green peninsulas reach out into the lake to create an irregular shore. Possibly these 'ears', (Wordsworth's name for them), were once mistaken for off-shore islands. In fact they are, like the islands of Derwentwater, the half-submerged summits of drumlins, that is ridges formed under the ice sheet.

51

Until being absorbed into Cumbria, Esthwaite, like Coniston, was wholly a Lancashire lake, though apparently deemed too insignificant to appear on the earliest of maps. The lake was, and still is, owned by the Sandys family of Graythwaite Hall on the road to Newby Bridge. Wordsworth knew it well during his Hawkshead schooldays: 'our little lake', round which he'd walk 'five miles of pleasant wandering', sometimes with a companion chanting verse in unison. Esthwaite and Rydal, being shallow, have normally always been the first lakes to freeze, and in winter the boys played hare and hounds across the ice, often skating far into the night. One of the poet's schoolfellows lost his life here in later years when the ice cracked and he was drowned. Nowadays a freeze only occurs once or twice in a decade.

Roads to Hawkshead and Wray bound either shore. To the west is Esthwaite Hall, originally the sixteenth-century home of the Sandys, and Esthwaite Lodge, now a Youth Hostel, where lived the historian Alcott Beck. Certainly, even the tourist whose only knowledge of Esthwaite is a motorist's impression, will be rewarded by a fair picture, for to borrow De Quincey's words, Esthwaite is 'a lovely scene in its summer garniture of woods'. Esthwaite, it must now be emphasised, deserves more than such a passing acquaintance.

Ancient Hawkshead is near, rather than by, the lake, and proceeding from there on foot the lake is approached by a short stroll through the meadows. At the head is the reeded pool known as Priest's Pot. Once it was the vivarium of the Furness Monks who, prior to Henry VIII's confiscation of their land, were the medieval owners of the fishery. Rather more evocative is the legend attributing the pool's name to its holding 'as much as a thirsty priest would like to drink in good ale'.

Speedboats have never been allowed to disturb the peace of Esthwaite, and its serenity appeals to the fishermen who frequently stay in Hawkshead, or Near and Far Sawrey—the prefix denotes 'near' or 'far' from Hawkshead. The angler hoping for perch or pike is usually well rewarded. Roach, not common to the Lakes, have been introduced into Priest's Pot, while Esthwaite trout have a reputation for being delicious.

All the lakes were formed at more or less the same time as a result of the retreating of the ice sheets following the glacial era. Glaciers flowed down the mountains, and rather than widening the valleys, cut more deeply into them. They gouged out troughs to form the basins of the lakes, blocking the exits with glacial debris. Naturally in the intervening period from then until now, roughly 10,000 years during the latter part of which man's influence was felt, changes have taken place. These changes are far more apparent in the southerly lakes where the surrounding land has lent itself to farming and increased habitation. This has led to greater development in the aquatic life, and as a term of distinction biologists, following the lead of Dr. Pearsall, describe them as the 'evolved' lakes. Esthwaite, with sheltered bays and a depth of only 47 ft., is the most 'evolved' or productive of all. So, providing ample food in addition to plenty of protective cover for nesting in the extensive beds of rush and sedge, it harbours a wider variety of waterfowl than is seen on most of the other lakes. Quarrelsome coot edge in and out of the reeds, where a moorhen lets out a hoarse croak. A heron may flap its heavy wings overhead, sandpipers call and Canada geese sail close inshore. If the presence of the human species proves too much for them, some of the Windermere duck use Esthwaite as a retreat.

Most interesting of all the regular bird life seen on Esthwaite are the great-crested grebes, diving to reappear so far away that it always surprises, however familiar a sight it may be. The crested grebes, common enough on the reservoirs of southern England, have only nested on Esthwaite since 1908. Their special significance is that, apart from Blelham Tarn, they rarely breed on any of the other Lakeland waters. Only sheltered Esthwaite offers the material and seclusion required to build their floating nests. It is estimated that a pair of grebes consumes a total of 300 lbs of food a year; this they take from Esthwaite mostly in fish, but with no objection to the odd newt or tadpole. In winter they may be joined by other diving duck, goldeneye, pochard, and tufted duck which turn up on several of the lakes.

Esthwaite makes no demands upon our energy, and we may wander part-way round its shore. Its rich waters, taking their colour from the sky, are fringed by a pattern of woods and flower-strewn meadows. Esthwaite is there to be admired, or fished, if the necessary permit has been obtained. It has a haunting, endearing charm which, long after we have left it, will 'flash upon that inward eye which is the bliss of solitude'.

Hawkshead, its 'village gown', has a medieval character distinguishing it from all other Lakeland towns. The foundation of its former importance, an importance which cannot be overestimated, lay with the Cistercian monks. Mention of the town occurs in the records of Furness Abbey, at the beginning of the thirteenth century, when a manor house was established at Hawkshead Hall. The monks held the manor for four hundred years, and the life of Hawkshead was focused on the trading of wool. The woollen industry has always been vital to the economy of the Lakes, and right up to the nineteenth century, woollen goods were despatched from Hawkshead by way of the pack-horse trail, to be ferried across Windermere.

No absolute boundary of the lands held by the monks was defined. Roughly it was between Windermere and Coniston, and from Elterwater in the north to the southern tips of the two lakes where they join the Leven and the Crake; the land which came to be known as High Furness. A visible link with these monastic landowners, with whom the history of Windermere, Coniston and Esthwaite is inextricably interwoven, is the Old Courthouse at the foot of Hawkshead Hill, the only surviving remnant of the manorial buildings.

Since 1968 it has housed a seasonal exhibition relating to the Lakeland way of life. Under the Courtroom's massive timbers are displayed, with pleasing ingenuity, the tools of farmer, spinner and weaver, with their skills fused in an historic piece of cloth of a traditional pattern woven about 1760. Differing alcoves recall other crafts, such as swill, or basket making, by which the men and women of the valleys earned their livelihood. In Hawkshead itself, with its narrow twisting streets and cobbled ways, odd corners, cottages with overhanging upper storeys and open spinning galleries, it is not dif-

Old Courthouse, Hawkshead

ficult to picture the town peopled with those industrious crafts-
men of bygone days.

The buildings huddle together as if for protection.
Wordsworth sealed the fame of both Archbishop Sandys'
Grammar School of 1585, the foundation house of which is a
feature of the town, and the decorative cottage of Anne Tyson,
with whom he lodged. Watching over Esthwaite and built of
local stone the church is no longer the same as when the poet
wrote:

> '*I saw the snow-white church upon her hill*
> *Sit like a throned lady sending out*
> *A gracious look all over her domain.*'

In his time it had been rough-cast to keep out the damp,
and white-washed. Later this was removed, and the church
regained a sterner aspect, more commanding than 'gracious'.

Devotees of Beatrix Potter may recognise the minute National Trust information centre as Tabitha Twitchett's shop.

Until May 1974 motoring through Hawkshead required a skill not far short of that required to negotiate the Wrynose Pass. The ancient walls of Thimble Hall and the cottage aptly nicknamed 'Bend or Bump', around which not only cars but buses and heavier traffic had to steer with extreme caution, were subject to constant battering. For residents and sight-seers alike, traversing the centre of Hawkshead was fraught with hazard. The planners, who one is tempted to feel might have acted long before, have at last built a short relief road to by-pass the centre, and Hawkshead, freed from its congestion breathes again.

3

CONISTON WATER

Coniston Water, dominated by the noble presence of the Old Man, has been the focal point of a diversity of men and events. The Norsemen named this southerly lake Thurston Water, the monks of Furness netted its fish, and managed the neighbouring farms and forests. Iron ore was transported to the lakeside bloomeries, and charcoal burners established their hutments close by. It captured the heart of Ruskin, and witnessed the last tragic attempt of Donald Campbell to break yet another water-speed record.

In medieval days the fishing rights of a lake were of major importance; in the thirteenth century, when Coniston was owned partly by William de Lancaster and partly by the influential Abbots of Furness, the monks were allowed the use of one boat and twenty nets. This was about the time that the first bloomeries were set up near the lake to smelt the iron ore transported by pack-horse and boat from local mines, and the large-scale felling of trees for charcoal began.

Mining, which if mooted as a current enterprise within the boundaries of any National Park would stimulate conservationist wrath, has had a long-term influence on Coniston, village and lake. The medieval iron-ore industry, furthered by the monks, was followed by the opening up of the copper mines in the Elizabethan era.

Refining of the copper on the banks of Church Beck resulted in 'muddy and corrupt waters' being carried into the lake. Inevitably the fish suffered. Many were said to have been poisoned by the polluted water. Only when the mining ceased entirely did the fishery revive.

Coniston Water

The bloomeries, of which relics remain, were generally situated at a short distance from the lake shore, or near a stream. There were many sites over the fells between Coniston and Windermere. Water was essential for cooling the tools, and also because traditionally the smelters were said to have a prodigious thirst.

With the eighteenth-century innovation of iron furnaces, notably at Backbarrow in the Leven Valley and by Penny Bridge over the Crake, the Coniston bloomeries were abandoned. The charcoal burners, who had supplied the bloomeries with fuel, transferred their trade to the furnaces, and from 1764 onwards to gunpowder mills as well. Slowly the number of pitsteads decreased, but it was not until the end of the 1930s that they vanished completely. A fact which all readers of Arthur Ransome's *Swallows and Amazons* will know full well:

> *'A great wood ran up the hillside on the eastern shore of
> the lake—Far up it they could see smoke curling slowly*

above the trees, a thin trickle of smoke climbing straight up . . . .'

Such a whirl of grey smoke usually indicated the presence of a charcoal burner in the coppice woods, where the necessary timber was so abundantly at hand. Bound to keep what are now termed anti-social hours, he frequently took his family with him, keeping them occupied making besoms, or yard brooms, from birch twigs. A temporary home, shaped like a wigwam, and constructed of branches and bracken was set up, and the felling began. The cut wood, stacked up in a mound,

Coppice Wood in Spring

was covered with turf and soil to block out the air. Then glowing gently, it underwent a slow charring process lasting at least twenty-four hours, after which it was thoroughly doused and raked out. The chance of a sudden burst of flame made the presence of stream or lake vital. Also, doubtless working amid smoke and dust the charcoal burners needed to quench their thirst as frequently as the smelters.

Unlike the Keswick mining, which lasted for no longer than a century or so, the Coniston copper mines, honeycombing the mountain sides, were worked until the mid-nineteenth century. A stroll up to Coppermines Valley reveals all the evidence of the deserted workings, where the abandoned shafts and spoil heaps tell their own tale.

Consequently when, in 1857, the Furness Railway was extended to run from Broughton-on-Furness, through Torver to Coniston; the location of Coniston Station (closed 1957) was nearer mountains than lake. The newly-opened railway was not, like the track to Lakeside and Windermere, solely an invitation to holidaymakers. The authorities also bore in mind the transport of copper, up till then carried down the lake by barge. Nevertheless, it was in imitation of Windermere's railboat excursions from Lakeside that the *Gondola* was introduced to Coniston Water.

Coniston welcomed the 84 ft. *Gondola* with much jubilation on her launching from Coniston Old Hall, just a couple of years after the opening of the station. At a cost of £1,100 she had been designed by Sir James Ramsden to carry 200 passengers. From then on, except for the years of World War I, she was in more or less continuous service until 1939. In 1908, she was joined by a sister ship, the *Lady of the Lake*. It was intended that she should replace the *Gondola*, but as the public showed a marked preference for the older boat, they both remained in service. The *Lady* was eventually broken up in 1950. The service ended, but the *Gondola* was not forgotten. A model, constructed by Captain Hamill, her Captain for fifty years, is in the Ruskin Museum, and the original boat is anchored near the reed beds at the southern end of Coniston Water. Coniston has always been proud of this historic craft of which Captain Hamill once said, 'There are few places on Coniston Lake where I could not put the prow into the green fields while the stern was in deep water.' Quite recently a local resident undertook the task of renovating her. Regrettably, before he had finished, vandals undid the work of restoration, and the last time we saw her the *Gondola* was a partial wreck sinking low in the water. Let us hope that Coniston will come to her rescue, for the graceful *Gondola*, the oldest steam yacht in Lakeland, made a felicitous contribution to the history of the lake.

Another original nineteenth-century craft to emerge from the boathouse at Coniston Hall, now the headquarters of the Coniston Sailing Club, was John Ruskin's *Jumping Jenny*. Ruskin, living at Brantwood on the east shore, asked William Bell to build the boat, but the design was Ruskin's own — 'she's my first essay in marine architecture and boat builders near and far approve.' From his intimate knowledge of the Continental lakes he modelled the bow on the boats of Lake Garda, gave it a narrow stern, and the whole was built of larch-wood. This, Ruskin believed, was the ideal hull for a lake boat. He christened her *Jumping Jenny* after Nanty Ewart's boat in Scott's *Redgauntlet*. Scott had been a literary hero since childhood.

The fate of the *Jumping Jenny* had not been left to chance. She has a dry mooring in the coachhouse at Brantwood, together with Ruskin's other forms of transport, his carriage and his bath-chair.

Other celebrities have had associations with Coniston; Turner and De Quincey both stayed at the *Black Bull;* Tennyson honeymooned at Tent Lodge; Coniston Old Hall, that splendidly chimneyed house, was the home of the Flemings; but Ruskin's long connections and enduring love for the place predominate. Nevertheless, as the twentieth century has progressed, his fame has faded, though the reforms he advocated, smokeless zones, green belts, and town planning, are now universally accepted.

Ruskin, writer, critic, artist, philosopher, who had a profound influence on Victorian taste, was born in London in

Brantwood

1819, the son of a prosperous sherry importer. Frequent journeys north with his parents as a boy, had given him an intimate knowledge of the Lake District. A passion for writing verse, a talent his father encouraged by paying him one penny for every twenty lines, expressed itself in *Iteriad,* an account of three weeks spent in the Lakes in 1830. With the *Low Wood Inn* at Windermere as their base, the Ruskin family, true to the manner of their time, toured the Lake counties with commendable thoroughness. On the day they journeyed to Coniston a storm overtook them, and the driver of their carriage drove at such speed that he almost tumbled them into the lake. A recognised characteristic of these inland waters is the urexpected rapidity with which a surface as smooth as the proverbial mill-pond may be whipped up by a sudden storm. On Coniston, in the fiercest of winds, the waves may rise as high as five feet. All in all it was:

'. . . . . . . rather an unlucky time
For giving a taste of the grand and sublime.'

They were forced to seek shelter at the *Waterhead Inn,*
where they 'dined upon taties and fine potted char'. The inn,
famed for its char, was not on the site of the present *Waterhead Hotel,* but in a field very close to the head of the lake, and
was destroyed by fire some thirty years later. After his marriage to Effie Gray, Ruskin spent his honeymoon in Keswick.
He did not then return to the Lakes for nineteen years, a long
absence, during which, with the marriage unconsummated,
Effie divorced him to marry the painter Millais. During this
time Ruskin, who was a prolific worker, achieved wide renown.

Eventually in 1871, two years after he was appointed the
first Slade Professor of Fine Art at Oxford, the dire effects of
overwork led to illness, and his thoughts returned to the Lakes
— 'I feel I should get better if I could lie down in Coniston
Water,' he wrote. It was fortunate for him, and for Coniston,
that at the very moment when he needed such solace, he was
able to buy Brantwood from William Linton, without seeing it
and solely on the reputation of its view across the lake. Linton
was a good engraver, and his wife, Elizabeth Lynn Linton, a
novelist. They had corroborated in producing a guide to the
Lakes. Later they parted, and thus enabled Ruskin to purchase their cottage for £1,500. 'Cottage' was the correct
description at that time, and its new owner found it 'old,
damp, decayed; smoky-chimneyed and rat-riddled'. He immediately set about renovating and enlarging.

The view was all important; a turret room, its windows lat-
ticed to resist strong winds and storm, was one of the first
additions. It enabled him to gaze upon the widest possible prospect of lake and mountain.

*'Yesterday an entirely perfect summer light on the Old
Man. Lancaster Bay all clear: Ingleborough and the great
Pennine fault as on a map. Divine beauty of western
colour on thyme and rose . . . . .'*

So he described the outlook on a day in June; and in mid-winter: 'Coniston lake shone under the calm clear frost in one marble field as strong as the floor of Milan Cathedral.' At Brantwood, to which initially he only returned intermittently from lecturing and travelling in Europe, he was joined, and cared for, by his cousin, Joan Severn, and her husband Arthur, a water-colour artist.

John Ruskin won the affection of the people of Coniston, who overcame their native reserve with all 'off-comers', as they began to appreciate his genuine interest in his neighbours, his love of children and his natural behaviour. 'He was fond of iverything in t'dale', a Coniston man told Rawnsley. Ruskin's ardent belief in the value of true craftsmanship led to a revival of spinning and weaving in the farmhouses of the Lake District. It was his influence which encouraged Rawnsley, both a friend and a disciple, to found the School of Industrial Art in Keswick.

Once a year Ruskin, overcoming his reluctance to admit the efficiency of steam power, would hire the *Gondola* to take himself and the residents of his house down to the *Lake Bank*

A quiet sail off Torver

Hotel, where they would stay while the annual spring-cleaning of Brantwood was in progress. Such domestic upheaval was too much for Ruskin and he only returned home when order had been restored.

Temperamentally John Ruskin was not a serene man; his private life was barren and unhappy, and towards the end the balance of his mind was sadly disturbed. At Brantwood on the east shore of Coniston Water, which he loved, he attained what measure of contentment was possible for such a man. Returned to the land of his boyhood excursions he responded to the unhurried waters of the lake, and the tranquillity of the equally unhurried way of life in the dale. When, in 1900, after a severe attack of influenza, he died, he was buried as he would have wished, in the little graveyard at Coniston. It was Ruskin's friend and biographer, W.G. Collingwood, who designed the tall commemorative cross of local stone. Collingwood was a noted authority on the Lake District, and his novel *Thurstein of the Mere* is based on Coniston Water during the Viking period.

Brantwood, associated in earlier times with the Sandys of Esthwaite, and Gerald Massey, the poet, was inherited by the Severns. Later it was purchased by J. Howard Whitehouse, a keen admirer of Ruskin and collector of his works. Since 1955 the house, interesting rather than beautiful, has been within the care of an Educational Trust, and is occupied as an adult residential centre and for other extra-mural activities. The house, with its collection of Ruskiniana, and the grounds are open to the public.

From the shrubbery and garden modern Brantwood has followed the example of others, and routed a nature trail through its 250 acres; though the manager prefers to describe it as a 'woodland walk'. Here are bloomery and charcoal burners' sites, and on the higher slopes above the woodland, the lonely farmhouse of Lawson Park. The term 'Park' derives from the days of the monks, masters of sheep husbandry, who enclosed areas of these wild fells, converting barren land to pasture to get precious wool. Further south Parkamoor and Water Park reflect the same origin. There is a sight of Grizedale Forest (where the Forestry Commission has its deer museum and splendid Forest Theatre), and the tumbling falls of Beck Leven.

At the highest point, 750 ft., is a panoramic view across to the dark buttress of Dow Crag, the Old Man and their companion summits. Almost to the sea, Black Coombe, formed from some of the oldest rock of all, rises over the Duddon Estuary. Always, below in the valley, is the shimmering level of Coniston Water.

The lake, 5½ miles long and 1 mile wide, has the typical finger shape of the ice-eroded valleys. It has just two islands, both small. Pottery and other traces discovered on Peel Island suggest it was once used as a medieval refuge. The fells of Furness, and the bracken-clad commons of Torver, threaded by a spate of running becks, slope down to the shore. Yewdale and Church Beck bring down their quota of water from the Coniston Fells; and to the south, where the Crake takes away the surplus, there are wider bays, reeded shores and the stern mountain tableau at the head of the lake gives way to a more pastoral view.

Coniston has no ferry and the few residents near the lake shore ferry themselves to and fro. At the landing stage by Church Beck, row-boats, all lovingly christened Bess, Stella, Jean, after a wife, a daughter, or a girl friend, wait on the beach to be hired by the hour, the day, or the week. A boatman in his long boots lies full length on the shingle re-varnishing his boat; a gull surveys the world from the top of an unclothed mast. So it might be on a weekday in spring.

Even before the real holiday-makers arrive in force a fine week-end tempts hundreds of day-trippers into the Lake District National Park. The birds of the lake, the cormorants of Fir Island, and the duck, will have to share their water with the yachts, the inflatable dinghies and the water skiers. The wagtails and the sandpipers will no longer have the series of pebbled bays to themselves.

Divers arrive equipped to go 'scratting'. At Waterhead we watched a couple who, after a lengthy search, eventually emerged from the water bearing two bottles. Despite being muddy and lined with pondweed they were in mint condition, uncracked, not even chipped. Two empty green glass bottles of pre-1913 vintage, so their retrievers informed us with a glow of satisfaction: 'Washed and polished they'll look very pretty with all the rest.' There spoke the true collector; one man's litter had become another man's treasure.

A diver never knows what he may discover in his underwater sessions, and the members of a sub-aqua club, exploring the depths of Coniston, one day brought to the surface a farmer's cart. About twenty-eight years previously, a local farmer had stationed his cart in the shallows to allow the spokes to swell. When he returned the cart had sunk from sight; which is just one instance of how sharply the lake bed shelves.

The major road, west of Coniston through Torver, only skirts the lake briefly, near Brown Howe. The lovely East of Lake Road from Monks Coniston, shaded by the leafy decoration of the lower fells, moves in harmony with the water's edge, from which it rarely strays. There are glimpses of the lake through the narrow boundary of shore trees on the one

Divers at Waterhead

Landscape with lambs, Monk Coniston

hand, and dappled light flickering through the casual canopy of leaf and branch on the other. Sheep scramble heedlessly on to the tarmac now and again, needing to be persuaded back to safer ground: a hazard of most Lake District roads. In the Lake District sheep are everywhere. Swaledales and Border Leicesters have now joined the local Herdwicks. No one knows how the grey Herdwicks arrived. The fact that there is no similar breed in Scandinavia tends to dispose of the theory that they accompanied the Norsemen. Semi-wild, they have a toughness and an agility which allows them to survive on the high and rugged fells. They are possessed of an extraordinary instinct by which they remain on those fells where they were reared. If they do stray away, they always return. They abide by their own invisible boundaries.

Previously, that is before local government reorganisation, Lancashire claimed Coniston wholly as its own. In spirit it still does. But generally speaking Coniston has not received the literary acclaim of the other lakes. It did not capture the imagination of the poets in quite the same way as Windermere and Derwentwater. As Lancashire's local lake, to the world at large it was never as accessible as Windermere. Tourists from the south having reached Newby Bridge or Bowness usually continued north towards the central lakes and higher mountains. For most travellers, reaching Coniston entailed a diversion by means of the Windermere Ferry, and the seven-mile road over High Furness.

Perhaps now, Coniston is glad that Wordsworth chose to live elsewhere, and that only in the last hundred years has its lake received notable literary and other far-reaching association. But to those who grew to know it well Coniston Water always had an abiding charm.

In this century, because as a boy he fell in love with Coniston where he had spent most of his holidays, 'in or on the lake, or on the hills above it', Arthur Ransome could not help writing *Swallows and Amazons*, and all the adventures which followed. Through him countless children grew up knowing the district of the Lakes without ever having been there. Ransome knew how to tell a story, and his own delight in the Lakes is spelt out on every page. He altered the geography as if allowing a fictitious earthquake to redispose the natural features. It matters not that Wild Cat Island corresponds with Ramp Holme in Windermere—although not exactly, for is it not Peel Island in Coniston that Ransome so lovingly describes? It was in fact one day when Ransome himself was sailing on Windermere that the *Amazons* were born. A small craft swung round Ramp Holme manned by two young girls in tasselled caps; and this one fleeting glimpse, for Ransome neither saw them again nor knew who they were, provided the inspiration for Nancy and Peggy Blackett, that innocent, adventure-loving pair of *Amazons*, only recently transferred to the colourful media of the cinema. Ransome's own adoration of the lakes, Coniston in particular, was such that on arrival he would run down to dip his hands in the water and wish, as if the lake held a touch of magic.

Unlike Bowness and Keswick, Coniston village has escaped

Yewdale Crag

expansion, and the paraphernalia of tourism. Essentially it
has remained a village. Situated at the head of the lake it has
derived its livelihood from the mountains, formerly from copper, and now to a lesser extent from the slate quarries. At first
the green slates, brought down precariously by sledge, only
supplied local demand. As transport became easier, their fame
spread to wider horizons. Today, slate quarrying is an important Lakeland industry, and the showrooms of the Broughton
Moor Slate Company are one of Coniston's tourist attractions.

The grey village of Coniston is clustered about Church
Beck. There is the track to Coppermines Valley; the church
with its beginnings dating back to 1586; the *Black Bull* known
to Turner, who made his mountain studies near Coniston; the
Sun linked with the Campbells, and tucked behind the library
in the shadow of Yewdale Crag is the Ruskin Museum. A
museum by no means solely concerned with Ruskin, as
Brantwood is, but allowing considerable space for exhibits
concerned with village and lake. The Wine Shop and Restaurant in Lake Road treasures the steering-wheel used by Sir Mal-

colm Campbell in setting up two water speed records, and on the village green is the simple memorial to his son, Donald.

It was in 1939 that Sir Malcolm Campbell sped out over the lake in his latest *Bluebird,* established a new world speed record of 141.74 mph and brought the name of Coniston Water before the eyes of the world. In that same year the country was plunged into war, and Coniston was to see no more record breaking until 1956.

Sir Malcolm died in 1948, and it was not till then that Donald, always a devoted admirer of his father, seriously considered following in his footsteps. Having decided to take up the challenge he was fortunate in having Leo Villa, his father's chief mechanic, as both friend and adviser. From 1949 Coniston grew accustomed to the periodic appearance of *Bluebird* making trial runs down the lake. All the Campbell boats were named *Bluebird.* In 1951 one of them was lost when, travelling at 170 mph, she hit a floating log and both Campbell and Leo Villa had a lucky escape as the boat sank.

Although Donald Campbell's first world record of 202.32 mph was set up on Ullswater in 1955, after that Coniston, its straighter shape making it a more suitable sheet of inland water, became the regular testing ground. For some years the names of Coniston and Campbell were synonymous.

The village, delighted to have another Campbell in its midst, supported him with willing offers of assistance. Connie Robinson and her husband, the friends he had made at the *Black Bull,* were now the proprietors of the 200 year old *Sun,* the recognised base of the *Bluebird* team. On each occasion that a new attempt was to be made, the attention of the sporting world was focused on Coniston.

The lake, peaceful haunt of fisherman, was caught in the glare of publicity. With Campbell came engineers and mechanics. In their wake followed all the representatives of the modern B.B.C. reporters, press-men, television and camera crews and, naturally, a host of interested spectators. Four records were broken in as many years. By 1959 *Bluebird* had shot down the water of Coniston at a speed of 260.35 mph.

Then there was a lull during which the energy, skill and cou-

The Sun Hotel

rage of Donald Campbell were occupied elsewhere in pursuit of the land speed record. Not until 1966 did he once again return to the Lake District. His aim was to drive his jet-boat along the surface of the lake at a speed of 300 mph.

In November 1966 Coniston, having closed its doors for the winter, re-opened them to welcome their hero, Donald Campbell, and his attendant retinue. Everyone had to be accommodated, fed and refreshed, and as many weeks were to pass before the attempt took place, commercially it was an off-season bonus for the village.

After certain difficulties in manoeuvring her transportation along the narrow lanes between Greenodd and Coniston, *Bluebird* arrived at the lake shore copiously wrapped in blue plastic sheeting. Trouble with the engine, gusty winds and tempestuous rain postponed the attempt several times. Days and weeks passed, and Coniston became acclimatised to the unseasonal crowds and the cars which brought expectant sightseers to the lake.

It was not until January 4th 1967, after the *Bluebird* contingent had occupied Coniston for sixty-four days, that Donald Campbell made his final tragic run. Those who watched that morning can only guess at what really happened. Arthur Knowles, who was present throughout all the preparatory weeks, tells how *Bluebird* flashed away down the lake, passed Peel Island, and turned to come back close to the eastern shore. Suddenly she left the surface of the lake, shot up into the air, plummeted down and vanished 'in a vast eruption of water'.

What exactly went wrong is not known. The cause of the accident still gives rise to speculation. Some time later Campbell's shoes, helmet and life-jacket floated to the surface. Royal Navy Divers went down again and again, and a proportion of the wreckage was eventually retrieved, but no trace of his body was ever found. It was estimated at the time that on her last run *Bluebird* had reach a speed of 328 mph. The world mourned the loss of a courageous man to whom the Queen gave a posthumous award for gallantry. There were many people in and around Coniston who had also lost a friend.

On the Hawkshead to Coniston road there was, as far back as 1598, a cottage called Tarnhouse. Nearby were three upland tarns. Just over a century ago a dam was built and they were merged into one. So Tarn Hows, man-made, and now the most frequented of all the Lake District tarns, came into being. Facing south the length of Coniston lake stretches away from you, and the scenic views across the Langdale Pikes, to

Red Screes and the Helvellyn range are part of Tarn Hows' manifold delights.

The idyllic setting in a hollow of the hills, with the shore and island conifers faithfully reflected in the looking-glass surface, and the moorhen scuttering through the water-lilies, all combine to make the easily accessible Tarn Hows over photographed and over visited. The National Trust has been faced with the dilemma common to all such popular beauty spots: how to prevent people spoiling the loveliness they come to see. More specifically at Tarn Hows the problem is how to cope with erosion caused by human feet. No words will explain the problem more lucidly than a few figures borrowed from the Trust's own report. On one August Bank Holiday over 6,000 people in 1,700 cars visited Tarn Hows. From mid-March to mid-November in 1972, 147,000 cars arrived bringing 515,000 people. Staggering as they may be, these figures do not, however, give the full picture.

The natural tendency at Tarn Hows is to seek the water's edge. So a count was made of those who walked along the waterside paths. Only one-tenth walked all the way round, one-fifth walked part way, and the rest stayed close to their cars.

Tarn Hows

The areas suffering greatest damage by erosion were thus those nearest the car parks. It has been proved that in some habitats, although many thousands of pairs of feet may pass over an area in a year no harm may result. But, if even a hundred pass in the space of an hour, all vegetation may be killed. To counteract the damage unwittingly caused at Tarn Hows small areas at a time are being restored.

All of which substantiates the point that even at the peak of the season it is still possible to avoid the crowds by walking only a short distance away from the honeypot areas. There is no need to take the car to Tarn Hows at all. It is easily reached on foot, being only two miles from either Coniston village or Hawkshead.

Somehow the true spirit of Lakeland evades beautiful Tarn Hows, and only on returning to the less attended coppice woods above Coniston, is it fully recaptured.

4

GRASMERE AND RYDAL WATER

The Vale of Grasmere is on the edge of the softer, southern landscape, before the mountain architecture is cast in sterner mould. Grasmere and Rydal Water are tranquil lakes, and in their size, or lack of it, lies the essence of their perfection.

Rydal is the smaller, three-quarters of a mile long and no more than a quarter of a mile at its widest extent. Affectionately called 'Reedy Rydal', its reeds, flourishing in the shallow water, grow higher than a man.

The mile long shore of Grasmere, below the steep ascent of Silver How, is just about double its width. Pastures fringe the shore in a brilliant patchwork of greens. Yet the explanation of its name as a 'lake of grassy shores' is too simple to be thought correct. More likely Grasmere, known earlier as *Grismere*, was the 'lake of the pigs', from the Norse *griss*, for pig, for swine were pastured in the valleys in pre-Norman times.

Whether gazing upon it from the shore, or rowing out to laze upon its banks, everyone falls in love with Grasmere's single island, where Dorothy Wordsworth watched the frolicking lambs. Over a century later Chiang Yee, the *Silent Traveller*, journeyed across the world from China and was enraptured by the 'little island in the middle of the lake, of a bewitching and magical colour, purple and blue—and shining in the sun'. Now I am told the farmer no longer rows his sheep over the water to crop the island's turf. The island is enchanting with its stone boathouse and sprinkling of trees, each with space to breathe and display its characteristic shape twice over, the slender pine, the bowing thorn and skirted chestnut.

To separate Grasmere and Rydal Water from the Wordsworths is as impossible as to divide the daffodils from the soil which nourished them.

The umbrella phrase 'The Lake Poets' covers the élite band of William and Dorothy Wordsworth, Coleridge, and Southey, who were later joined by their admirers De Quincey and Professor Wilson. Wordsworth, born in Cockermouth, schooled in Hawkshead and in 1799 at the age of twenty-nine, after Cambridge and his French adventuring, drawn irresistibly back was, of course, the lodestar who drew the others to the land of the English Lakes.

Anyone who is not familiar with Dorothy's *Grasmere Journal* has an exquisite experience in store. There is no more opportune time to open its pages than before, or when, visiting 'Our own dear Grasmere'. In her commonplace notebooks, using the quill pens of her time, and in an untidy hand, smudged here and there, she wrote a faithful account of all the daily incidents, the tending of the garden, the frugal meals, and the fascinating trivia of life in a village. All that she could note about 'her beloved brother' she did, for William was always at the forefront of her mind. But, intensely alive to the natural sights and sounds of the countryside, she never missed a flower that blossomed, a robin chasing a butterfly, the deepening colour of a leaf.

Boating on the lake till nearly midnight, Dorothy and William rejoiced in 'the rich reflections of the moon'. The lakes, so constant an inspiration, had a practical value to the Wordsworths, and to the rest of the village, as a source of food, especially in the Dove Cottage days. Fishing for bass and pike was one of William's regular occupations and in his time, of course, nearby Thirlmere was free to be fished as well. Not that they were always successful, as Dorothy was careful to record. Collecting pike-floats from Robert Newton at the *Red Lion* they took Mr. Gell's boat out one June day but 'we caught nothing—it was extremely cold'. Five days later they were in luck and the *Journal* reads, 'caught a pike 7½ lbs'. Not written originally for publication it is the complete unedited naturalness of Dorothy's *Journal* which has left for posterity an endearing and lucid picture of the day-to-day life at Dove

Dove Cottage

Cottage, and of the small community who lived and worked within access of Grasmere and Rydal.

It is currently more fashionable to read about Wordsworth than to read his poetry, the best of which was written at Dove Cottage. Not that the Wordsworths ever called it by the name derived from its earlier local importance as the *Dove and Olive Bough Inn;* to them it was always Townend. Somewhat to our surprise, not so many months ago, we saw and heard a tall, spectacled father pausing a few yards from the Wordsworths' old home, book in hand, reading lines from *The Prelude* aloud to his young sons. His sense of occasion was admirable; he read on presumably unaware that the boys' attention was being speedily diverted by the manoeuvres of a coach backing out of the narrow street. Who knows, in years to come they might remember their father's dedication?

For nine years the cottage was the Wordsworths' home, a home like many in the Lake District, with the larder placed so that a stream ran underneath to keep it cool. The rent was £8 a year. If the well which William dug in the garden ran dry, then water had to be carried in buckets from the village pump, or even, especially on the days of 'a great wash', from the lake. By 1808, the household which consisted of the singular *menage a trois*, Dorothy, William, and his wife, plus their first three children, truly needed more space. It was from Allan Bank, their next abode, that Dorothy busied herself preparing Dove Cottage for its new tenant, De Quincey, who was to occupy it for twenty-seven years.

De Quincey had written to Wordsworth a letter of youthful admiration at a time when the poet was quite out of fashion, and De Quincey, always a modest, unassuming man, kept his veneration to himself. So timid and lacking in self-confidence was he that twice, having been invited by Wordsworth to Grasmere, he travelled to the Lakes, but was unable to summon up sufficient courage to present himself. But he never forgot his eventual first visit to Dove Cottage.

On the morning after his arrival he came downstairs to see Miss Wordsworth making breakfast in the little sitting-room. 'No urn was there; no glittering breakfast service; a kettle boiled upon the fire and everything was in harmony with these unpretending arrangements.' Never had he entered so humble a home, and honouring Wordsworth, as in his youth he did, his respect was increased 'to the uttermost' by all he saw. Their eventual friendship waned for various reasons, but chiefly because of Wordsworth's attitude to De Quincey's marriage to Margaret Simpson, a local farmer's daughter. Dorothy wrote in her *Journal*: 'Mr. De Q. is married and I fear I may add he is ruined.' De Quincey was the son of a wealthy merchant and the difference in social class was, at that period of history, too important a factor to be overlooked, and although, despite Dorothy's prediction, the marriage turned out to be a happy one, De Quincey was deeply and irreconcilably hurt. Living in so small a community it must have been difficult for them to avoid meeting each other as they took their daily walks. It was the death of little Kate Wordsworth, for whom De Quincey had a most special affection, which finally severed their friendship. When he later wrote his own *Recollections of the Lake Poets* they were tainted by the hurt he was unable to forgive.

Thousands of visitors annually move through the small rooms of Dove Cottage accompanied by a guide relating the more hackneyed details of Wordsworth's life. Ten minutes or so later, having ticked it off the list, they do not always take the few extra steps down the road to the Museum, where the atmosphere of Grasmere a century and a half ago really does come alive. The Wordsworth Museum occupies the handsomely beamed barn of Sykeside, a farmhouse older than Dove Cottage, where lived Molly Fisher, servant to the Wordsworths. The exhibits cover a wider field than its name suggests, for although centred upon the letters, manuscripts and possessions of the poet, his family and friends, it also displays relics relating to the way of life of the village in bygone days. There is a wrestling belt won at the Rushbearing celebrations in 1850, a wooden bobbin, spinning wheel, char dish and differing leisters for spearing salmon and eels, products of the local smithy, and an impressive reconstruction of a farmhouse kitchen.

After Allan Bank (later the home of Canon Rawnsley and

his second wife, Eleanor) the Wordsworths had a brief tenancy of Grasmere Rectory, a house of tragic memories, where two of William's young children, Catherine and Thomas, died within a year. Finally in 1813 the Wordsworths settled in Rydal Mount, at which, as public viewing is a recent innovation, we might take a closer look.

The Mount, privately owned since the Poet's residence, came on the market in 1969, and was bought by his great granddaughter, Mrs. Mary Henderson, in conjunction with a Trust launched by her brother, Richard Wordsworth. Consequently it is the first local house to be owned by a Wordsworth, William having been a perpetual tenant.

Rydal Mount

Situated below Nab Scar the four-hundred-year-old farm-house was a home in less frugal days which saw its master elevated to Poet Laureate. We are no longer able to share the Wordsworths' lake view from Dove Cottage for houses intervene, but from the garden of the Mount, where many of the trees and shrubs were planted by William himself, there is the long view over Rydal Water and the valley of the Rothay which so delighted him. Dorothy wrote that their latest home was 'the nicest place in the world for children'. Derwent and Hartley Coleridge came, and the young Matthew Arnold from Fox How, and over a century later in the spring of 1974 local children gathered here to re-enact for television the occasion of William's seventy-third birthday.

Indoors, strolling through the poet's attic study, or his daughter Dora's bedroom with its uneven floor, there seems no more aura of the Wordsworths and their friends than in Dove Cottage. Perhaps too much has happened in the interim. Or maybe the spruce and meticulous arrangement reflects the character of Mary Wordsworth, whose name is heard the least. For it was she, Harriet Martineau tells us, who set such an example of comfortable thrift in the housekeeping of the Mount that 'the homes of the neighbours have assumed a new character of order and comfort'. When Dorothy succumbed to the illness which overwhelmed the last twenty years of her life and lived in a shadowy world of her own, 'sweet Mary' attended her most cheerfully.

Although they never materialised, ideas of building his own home did occupy William's thoughts from time to time; once when he was given some land near Applethwaite, north of Keswick, and again when the possibility of his tenancy ending arose and he bought the field beside Rydal Church, now known as Dora's Field. Previously it was called the Rashfield because of the rushes which grew there. Reached through Rydal churchyard this beautiful retreat is not really a field in the accepted sense, but a secret sheltered part of the hillside enhanced by stately trees and carpeted in spring by daffodils and bluebells.

The lines a poet is inspired to write draw the sightseers to a place; then commerce steps in and trades upon their coming. Grasmere village, off the main Ambleside road before it speeds on over Dunmail Raise to Kewick, is undeniably designed for tourists who include it in their Lakes tour with unfailing regularity. Within the yew-shaded grounds of the medieval church, all the familiar names are gathered together, William, Mary and Dorothy, Dora and her husband, Edward Quillinan, and Hartley Coleridge. Rarely are other names searched for in this graveyard beside the Rothay, but here too are remembered the Lake artist, William Green, and the Arctic explorer and naturalist, Sir John Richardson, who married one of the Fletchers of Lancrigg House.

The prominence of studios, handicraft shops and hotels causes a momentary query as to where the village does its routine shopping. If it is Grasmere you wish to see rather than your fellow men *en masse*, then avoid it at Easter and Bank Holidays when the world and his wife go sightseeing.

Even if the Wordsworth pilgrimage is not taken into account Grasmere still has the advantage of its central position, as all the large lakes can be reached within approximately a fifteen mile radius, and climbers set off for Helvellyn, Fairfield and the peaks, which are just about the centre of the National Park, High Raise. Who would visit Grasmere without setting foot upon one of the numerous tracks up Loughrigg, pausing every while or so to look back for a bird's-eye view of one or other of the two little lakes? One of the happy surprises of the Lake District is that round almost every other screen of rock a new water comes into view. From the differing summits of Loughrigg there is also a sight of Windermere, of Esthwaite and, at the western foot of the fell, the near-circle of Loughrigg Tarn.

The tarns, small blue landmarks on the map, attract the eye. Because most people like to walk towards a goal rather than just anywhere, they are a regular objective. Thus the walk from Grasmere to Easedale, a high, but not so lonely tarn, follows a much trodden path through meadows and on by the Sourmilk Gill to find the source 900 ft. up.

The picturesque Rushbearing ceremony commemorating

River Rothay linking Grasmere and Rydal

St. Oswald's Day, held annually on the Saturday nearest to
5th August, draws throngs of sightseers to Grasmere. Rushes
and reeds are gathered from the lakeside, flowers from the
meadows, ferns and greenery from the woods, to compose the
posies and emblems the children carry as they walk by the lake
and through the village eventually to lay their lovingly made
and decorative bearings within the church. Formerly the

rushes were strewn about the earthen floor for warmth. At the time when Wordsworth's children joined in the procession a custom which their father heartily approved, it was led by a fiddler, and the occasion has long been followed by the traditional gaiety of cakes and ale; the 'cake' in Grasmere being gingerbread. A full band, prepared for the photographer's lens and the television camera, leads the pageant today, but the gingerbread from the minute corner shop which was once the school, is still forthcoming.

Perhaps those same crowds, or similar ones, which wended their motorised way over the Raise, or crammed the road from Ambleside and the south, to be spectators at the Rushbearing will be back again a fortnight later for Grasmere's major event, the Sports, always held on the Thursday nearest to the 20th August. The outstanding contest is the celebrated Guides' Race to the top of Butter Crag. The speed of the fell-runners is extraordinary. They are a tough breed, typical of the Lakeland farmer stock from which they spring. Running up and down the fell slopes of Cumbria is an exercise they take for the sheer love of it. Certainly it is not for financial reward; the first price for the Grasmere Guides' Race is about £20. Tommy Sedgwick, British Fell Racing Champion, and the winner in 1973, took 10 minutes and 10 seconds to gain the top and 2 minutes and 56 seconds worth of leaps and bounds to come down; downhill with the risk of loose stones, rabbit holes and slippery patches being far the more treacherous run:

> *'And he looked like a shooting star almost*
> *As down the cliffs he sped.'*

I believe that the first Sheepdog Trials in the Lake District were held on Belle Isle, Windermere. Everyone nowadays associates them with Rydal Park where, again in August, the finest sheepdogs of the north country display their unerring skill.

Returning to the lakes, the complexities of their drainage system, or if that conjures up too prosaic a picture, the in-flow and out-flow, reveals an intriguing natural watercourse. A

85

lake is, in this context, a widening or expansion of the system through which the flow of water, fast moving in the mountain becks, slows down to become 'a standing water'. The water of Windermere, for instance, takes nine months to pass from one end of the lake to the other.

In the movement of the waters of the Central Lake District, the River Rothay plays a vital role. With its source in the shadow of Steel Fell, it serves the lakes well. After entering Grasmere from the north, it tumbles out again in the south east corner, and runs, crystal clear, under the trees below the foot of Loughrigg. Having fed the two small and lovely waters, it flows gently through the immortal Stepping Stones, to unite unite with the Brathay from Elterwater, and lose itself in Windermere.

Every now and again man takes a hand and adds his own refinements. Recent lengthening of the spillway from Grasmere and dredging of the river below has enabled flood water to get away quickly, but the reconstruction has also ensured that the level of the lake is sustained in dry spells. A fish-pass has been built into the spillway to help the salmon get up to spawn in the becks above the lake. Similarly, in Rydal it was

Stepping Stones, Rydal

realised that the matted growth of the famed 'plots of water lilies lifting up their target shaped leaves to the breeze' was impeding the flow. They had, with obvious regret, to be thinned out but, liking this shallow mere, are already reasserting themselves.

Though perch are plentiful in Grasmere (and there are also the expected eels, pike and trout) serious anglers, aware of the intense competition from photographers and sightseers, may not regard either lake as a first choice.

There is one small lay-by on the A591 in its otherwise non-stop skirting of both the lakes. This is beside Grasmere. So closely does the road hug Rydal's northern shore that some of the peace is lost, and only the wintering grey-lag geese prefer this side of the water. The traffic allows us but a hasty glance at the huge rock where Wordsworth pondered, or at Nab Cottage where holidaymakers now sleep under the roof which sheltered both De Quincey and Hartley Coleridge at differing times. Yet on the opposite shore, traffic forgotten, we can relax in the habitual calm of the placid mere where mallard and coot swim lazily towards the islands.

Let us explore Rydal from White Moss Common. In this

Nab Cottage

Footbridge at White Moss

marshy land between the lakes grow some of the characteristic plants of the Lake District, rushes the children gather for emblems, the cream blossoms of the meadowsweet, shining clumps of kingcups, bluebells, water lobelia. Also, in the vicinity of Rydal since the 1930s there has flourished a new flower with which the Wordsworths would not have been familiar. This is the tall sweetly-scented pink balsam, commonly called Policeman's Helmet. Unfortunately, its careless habit of overwhelming other waterside plants has brought it into disrepute with naturalists.

It was, by chance, at White Moss that we talked with one of the residents of the Lakes who act as Voluntary Wardens. Working from their homes they assist the regular staff whose Land Rovers may hove into sight anywhere within the boundaries of the National Park. The volunteers wear armbands and badges of identity. They are, like the staff, always willing to help with advice and direction, to guide and inform; but a major part of their duties is accomplished behind the scenes.

In their role as caretakers, the National Park Authorities are faced with considerable problems. Problems which increase annually since, with the opening up of major roads, and the M6 flying up the eastern boundary, the Lake District is now within three hours' driving distance of 20 million people.

The policy of all National Parks, and of the Trust, is to refrain from labelling the land with notice boards and signs, unless absolutely necessary. Yet one of the disadvantages of the term 'National Park' is that it is liable to misinterpretation. 'Park' in contemporary language implies land reserved for leisure and recreation. This is not entirely so. Conservation and preservation continue alongside farming, sheep rearing and forestry. With mutual respect there is no reason at all why the interests of a farmer, landowner and tourist should conflict.

As well as the Rothay and many literary memories, the two lakes currently share a pair of mute swans. We happened to see them preening their feathers on Grasmere's southern shore. Between October and April it is not unusual for the pair to be joined by whooper swans whose bugle-like whooping is heard over many of the lakes during the winter months. One winter, forty of these impressive birds were seen and heard trumpeting on Grasmere. Whereas a few of the Lakeland birds, such as the osprey, heron and kingfisher commonplace in Wordsworth's day, have sadly declined in numbers, or disappeared altogether, the whoopers have become more numerous in the last thirty years. Each of Rydal's miniature islands wears its own posy of trees. But it is long since the herons nested there. Possibly they moved away because the small lake was, at one time, overfished.

Towering on the north is Nab Scar, with the line of Red Screes on the distant horizon. To the north-west at the approach to Dunmail Raise is Helm Crag, its larger and lesser summit rocks known to the world as the Lion and the Lamb. On the slopes of Loughrigg, and unseen from the shore, is

Rydal Cave

Rydal Cave, sometimes referred to as the Giant's, or Cathedral Cave. A section of the hillside was once cut into to test the possibility of serious quarrying. Mercifully, after quite a sizeable excavation had been made it was decided not to continue, thus bequeathing to Rydal the largest cavern in the Lake District. The lofty, irregular walls rise up cathedral-fashion to the roof. On first entering each length of hanging slate, abandoned to its natural disarray, appears uniformly grey. Only as our eyes grow accustomed to the dimness of the light, do we become aware of the varying hues of pink and green and grey, of both a deeper and a lighter shade. Looking out from within the hillside, the entrance frames the buttress of Nab Scar, and on the floor a minnowed pool draws reflections from the sunlit boulders outside. Rydal Cave is damp and slippery, and should be treated with care, but it is surprisingly beautiful when the light is strong enough to reveal the subtle colouring of the slate.

On the periphery of Wordsworth's kingdom, and still in the centre of the Lake District, is the less publicised and beautifully-wooded Elterwater. Resembling a group of very shallow, elongated pools, it is sometimes called a tarn rather than a lake. The winding water, owned by the Trust, is a popular beauty spot before moving out of the world of the lakes into Langdale, where the names of Pike O'Stickle, Gimmer Crag and Pavey Ark spell seventh heaven to the mountaineers.

It was near Elterwater, during World War II that Kurt Schwitter, whose work may now be seen in the Tate Gallery, gained refuge after escaping from occupied Norway.

The biologists, who speak in tens of thousands of years, remind us that lakes are a transitory feature of the landscape. Elterwater is a clear illustration of their point. Fed by the insistent torrent of the Great Langdale Beck, and drained by the Brathay, it is the remnant of a former larger lake into which sediment encroached, pushing out into the water to form the present irregular outline. Imperceptibly the infilling continues, and in all probability at some unknown date in the future there will be no lake in Langdale at all.

The Norsemen called it *Elpt Vatn,* the lake of the swans, based on the original belief that the wilder wintering swans arrived here first. Swans do visit these random shores which, lately, have sheltered a newcomer to the regular bird life of the Lakes, the red-breasted merganser. These fish-eating diving ducks, with dishevelled crests and long, thin bills, have only been colonising the National Park since the 1960s, and may well be seen on Windermere, Coniston and other waters. Why they or the whooper swans have come no one really knows.

One of the first men to survey the English lakes was Jonathan Otley. Born in Grasmere in 1766, he spent most of his ninety years in Keswick. A basket maker and clock mender by trade, he studied to acquire wide renown as a geologist. His observations of Elterwater prompted him to remark that the trout fishery had been more or less annihilated by 'that voracious fish, the pike'. There are trout in the lake today, but there are no boating facilities, and fishermen will find better sport in deeper waters.

Elterwater village has forgotten the industrial workings of the gunpowder mill which once gained its power from the

Langdale Beck, and reveals a welcoming face to all who pass this way. A sycamore spreads its branches over the apron of green. Behind it is the village inn, the *Britannia*. Before it the track keeps course with the beck to the lake, and moving south the road will take us to Colwith Force.

Of the two outstanding falls in the immediate vicinity it is Skelwith, in the lovely valley of the Brathay, which most people visit. The Brathay falls over only 12 ft. of rock at Skelwith, but with a magnificent rush into a sea of foam. From Skelwith Bridge it is close enough to the road to be constantly admired.

Colwith has received less attention, yet has a magic of its own. Early in the morning, before the rest of the world is stirring, is the ideal time for Colwith. Then the walk up High Park is accompanied by bird-song and the eternal music of the falls. Suddenly, through the oak and sycamores, there it is cascading over 90 ft. in two falls, meeting briefly on a bed of rock to re-divide and splash over into the ravine. On it goes, dancing merrily over the stones. Even in time of drought it loses little of its vivacity. No wonder Professor Wilson, with Victorian licence, named it 'the Glory of Little Langdale, the Lady of the Woods'.

5

DERWENTWATER AND BASSENTHWAITE LAKE

Derwentwater is the fifth largest of the lakes, 3½ miles long, not more than 1¼ miles wide and with a depth of only 72 ft., less than half that of Coniston or Ullswater. Cradled by the mountains, adorned by wooded islands, and with miniature bays and promontories indenting its shore from Keswick to Lodore, from Great Bay to Nichol End, it shines like a resplendent jewel before the gates of Borrowdale.

The form of a lake, Wordsworth believed, was most perfect when, like Derwentwater, it least resembled a river 'when being looked at from any given point where the whole may be seen at once, the width of it bears such proportions to the length that, however the outline may be diversified by far-receding bays, it never assumes the shape of a river, and is contemplated with that placid and quiet feeling which belongs peculiarly to the lake ... '.

It is generally accepted that a lake should be viewed up the water to its head. Early guides detailed viewpoints or 'stations' such as Castlehead, or Catbells, where the prospect of Derwentwater and its guardian mountains is indeed sublime. Yet there is no more rewarding way of appreciating the lake in its entirety than from a boat.

From Keswick, launches circle the lake travelling alternately in opposite directions, and because they call on request at all, or any of the five jetty stops, Ashness, Lodore, High and Low Brandlehow and Hawse End, they serve a dual purpose. Firstly, to circumnavigate the lake, and secondly, as a ferry between any of the stages. This makes them an ideal vehicle

Landing Stage at Keswick

for an exploration of the lake. It is tempting to leave the launch at Ashness Gate for Watendlath or Walla Crag, at Hawse End to climb the ridge of Catbells, or seek the seclusion of the Newlands valley. Or, for the less energetic, merely to disembark at one stage and follow the shore path to pick up a boat at the next. But for now let us sail with the launch all the way round.

Picture a summer morning. One of those promising mornings when we rise and dress with eager speed, and do not dally. We are keen to be off and out. Breakfast conversation has an added sparkle. Flasks and sandwiches are packed up, and we are away.

The last remnants of mist are dispersing over the peaks of Borrowdale, and the Queen of the English lakes, smooth as silk today, displays her classic beauty. The serious fell walkers have vanished towards Seatoller and the Scafell range. Cars, seeming as if duty bound to cover the maximum number of

Lake District miles, leave and enter Keswick with increasing frequency. Already there are sightseers on Friar's Crag, and at the boating place the first launch of the day is about to depart.

Before we embark it is fitting to appreciate a slab of local green stone placed on the bank to ensure the name of Rawnsley, 'who greatly loved the fair things of nature', is not forgotten. As a co-founder of the National Trust, a Trust we now tend to take for granted, Hardwick Drummond Rawnsley was far ahead of his time.

Born in 1851 at Shiplake, Oxfordshire, educated at Uppingham and Balliol, he had his first living at Wray, near

Derwentwater from Friar's Crag

Hawkshead and was Vicar of Crosthwaite, Keswick from 1881-1917. As he walked beside Derwentwater, over the Coniston and Langdale fells, always intensely aware of the perpetual splendour of lake and mountain, he was moved to work towards its preservation for all time. Rawnsley came to be fondly regarded as the watchdog of the Lake District. When the Trust was founded he received from his friend Wilfred Lawson these light-hearted lines:

'In that beautiful spot Derwentwater
It is said that the sunshine grows shorter,
But the sun will come out, I haven't a doubt,
When Rawnsley declares that it oughter.'

How appropriate it is that the first Trust property in the Lake District was 108 acres under the slopes of Catbells on the western shore of Derwentwater. The Trust today cares for much of Derwentwater, its surroundings and all its islands, the largest of which, Derwent Isle, we see even before moving away from the jetty.

Covering seven acres, Derwent Isle has had an eventful life. The Norsemen called it Hestholm, and when later it formed part of the Furness Abbey estates it was known as Vicar's Island. Its most flamboyant period occurred in the eighteenth century, during Mr. Pocklington's residence. He was a man of eccentric ideas, who conceived the nucleus of a village on his island, complete with church and fort. Regattas were his liveliest extravagance, highly theatrical and noisy events when Derwentwater was transformed by a mock sea-battle. Peter Crosthwaite, founder of Keswick's museum, was the chosen 'Admiral', and a fleet of barges armed with small cannon—one may be seen in the local museum—besieged the 'Governor' on his island to the accompaniment of 'much discharge of musquetry'.

Whereas the majority of present-day sightseers seek peace as a relaxation from the shattering tempo of the metropolis, so, conversely, those who toured the Lakes during the Romantic era would have been vastly disappointed had they not heard the echoes from Mr. Pocklington's cannon, reverberate across the water.

Following the Pocklingtons the island was bought, reputedly on Wordsworth's recommendation, by Henry Marshall, a wealthy industrialist's son from Leeds whose three brothers, lured by the spell of the Lakes, had already settled in homes nearby. He enlarged the existing house on his island home, and discovered the absorption of bird-watching. During the Marshalls' nineteenth-century residence, every now and again the sound of a loud bell rang out across the water calling for their personal ferryman. Although in our own time Mr. Denis Marshall has given Derwent Isle into the Trust's protection, it is occupied by a tenant, and its privacy remains inviolate.

However, Friar's Crag, the first and famed landmark upon the eastern shore, is rarely free of the tourist's tread. No other lake possesses a promontory as superbly placed as this rocky outcrop, looking straight up to the head of the lake and the rugged summits of the highest mountains of the Lake District. The familiar words of Ruskin recalling the Crag, and his first visit to Derwentwater, reflect the lasting depth of childhood impressions:

> 'The intense joy that I had in looking through the hollow in the mossy roots, over the Crag into the dark lake, has associated itself more or less, with all twining roots ever since.'

The air is sweet below the Scots pines on Friar's Crag, and the beach at its foot, possibly used by the Furness Friars as a landing place, is now an established parade ground for Derwentwater's resident geese. In common with geese inhabiting any of the lakes it is impossible to know whether they are wild or feral, because since 1961 numbers of both the handsome black-headed Canada goose, and the native grey-lag have been introduced into the National Park. To the holidaymaker it matters only that they are an adornment of the lake.

The next isle that the boat skirts as it sails under Walla Crag to Ashness Gate, is Lord's Island. On its 6 acres the Radcliffes,

97

JOHN RUSKIN

MDCCCXIX – MDCCCC

THE·FIRST·THING
WHICH·I·REMEMBER
AS·AN·EVENT·IN·LIFE
WAS·BEING·TAKEN·BY
MY·NURSE·TO·THE·BROW
OF·FRIAR'S·CRAG·ON
DERWENTWATER·

Ruskin Memorial, Friar's Crag

manorial owners of Keswick to whom local mining had brought increased prosperity, chose to build themselves a mansion. During the Jacobite rising of 1715 James Radcliffe, second Earl of Derwentwater, was arrested for having sympathies with the Pretender. Pleas to save him were in vain, and he was eventually dispatched to the Tower and executed. Greenwich Hospital received his confiscated Derwentwater estates. The mansion on Lord's Island had been abandoned before this, about the time of the Civil War, and Radcliffe relics found their way into the town of Keswick.

The island itself was later purchased for the Trust as part of the memorial to Rawnsley.

The launch makes its first call at Ashness Gate, where the way leads through the oakwoods to the much photographed bridge at Ashness, and the bonus prospect of both the lakes of this valley, for beyond Derwentwater is Bassenthwaite lying under the slopes of Skiddaw. The wooded road to Watendlath pursues a narrow winding course, where a motorist needs to concentrate on his steering.

Such is the unpredictability of the Lakeland weather and so abruptly does it change that on our most memorable visit to Watendlath rain besieged us all the way. It gave us no respite for the picnic lunch we'd planned to eat beside the beck. We had to munch as we walked, transferring sausage rolls and sandwiches from pocket to mouth with increasing speed. Then, as we saw Watendlath ahead of us, the curtain of rain lifted.

The newly-washed cottages shone in the returning sunshine, the beck glistened as it escaped from the grass-edged tarn and hastened down to achieve its erstwhile fame at Lodore. A dipper, its head bobbing to and fro in the characteristic movement by which it earned its name, alighted on a rock below the bridge. Briefly the secluded hamlet displayed its charms for us alone.

Pack-horse bridges, of which Watendlath is probably the most famous, were built of local stone mostly between 1660 and 1760, when laden horses were the principal form of transport. Before they captured the frequent attention of the cam-

Pack-horse Bridge, Watendlath

era lens, Wordsworth referred to them as 'a pretty subject for the pencil'.

Swans glide over the dark waters of the tarn, pike lurk unseen, and chaffinches, dozens of them, are quick to perch upon the nearest boulder if visitors pause to picnic beside this upland mere. Like the blue tits at Rydal, they also flock around the land Watendlath has reserved for visitors' cars. In winter the male chaffinches, so brightly coloured, yet so common we take them for granted, have a habit of moving about in large flocks. At Watendlath I have seen twenty or thirty arrayed along the the leafless branches of a sycamore, posed as if competing with the bridge and the ducks for the photographer's attention.

Hugh Walpole, who, maybe unwisely, used real names to tell his *Herries Chronicle*, imagined in Watendlath the 'home' of Judith Paris. Sightseers still walk over the bridge asking, 'Which is *her* farm?' Rival claims have been settled, and only

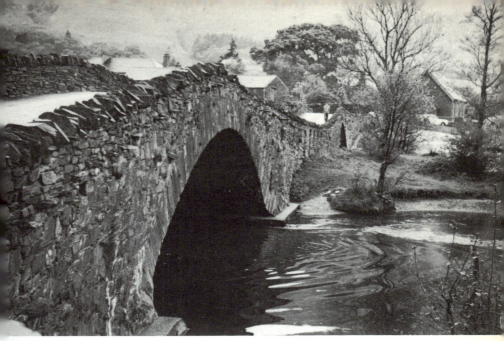

Bridge at Grange-in-Borrowdale

one, identified by a discreet plaque, currently asserts its right
to this distinction.

From Watendlath it is difficult to resist the pony track to
Rosthwaite, or the walk over Armboth Fell to Thirlmere, but
we must return to the lake and our launch as it sails towards
Lodore. It was from this landing that the forerunner of the
present Derwentwater motor launch service originated. In
1905 Mr. Harker, the then proprietor of the Lodore Hotel,
decided to run a service for the extra entertainment and conve-
nience of his guests. Mr. Harker's boats did not make a circular tour as today, but steered a criss-cross path from Lodore
to Brandlehow, then to Keswick, Portinscale and back to
Lodore. Harker was a man of initiative, and ran his boats, so
we are told, from electric batteries kept under the seats. He
recharged them from the Falls.

It is said you may catch a glimpse of Lodore from the
launch; however it is more than likely you will not. The cele-

brated cascade, well screened by trees, needs very heavy rain if it is not to be a disappointment. Tourists, seeing water sprinkling insignificantly over the rocks, think they have been misdirected. The image of a seething, foaming force cascading down 150 ft., between Gowder Crag and Shepherd's Crag, as when Southey's children asked him: 'How does the water come down at Lodore?' is normally more impressive than the reality.

Near Lodore, about 300 yards north of the mouth of Watendlath Beck, Derwentwater's Floating Island has invited curiosity and conjecture over the centuries. Generally seen only between June and September, its presence, or non-presence, was variously explained. Mystery touched this corner of the lake, conjuring up an island, and then causing it to vanish again. Harriet Martineau dismissed it summarily, 'The Floating Island ... has obtained more celebrity than it deserves.' But, as Miss Martineau must have been aware, the Floating Island was a legend. Tourists love a legend no less than the locals love to tell it.

Jonathan Otley was the first to use his enquiring mind on a thorough study of Derwentwater. One of his self-imposed tasks was to record the varying levels of the lake on the base of Friar's Crag. He it was who proffered the most likely, and widely accepted explanation of the island phenomenon, as an interwoven mass of submerged water plants driven to the surface by gases resulting from decomposition.

Leaving Lodore and its ultra-smart hotel, the launch crosses the mouth of the Derwent. The name Derwent, duplicated in river and lake, came in all probability from the Celtic *dwr-gwyn*, meaning clear water. After its long journey down from Borrowdale, the fair river with its enchanting birches, is graciously arched, twice over, by the bridge at Grange. Grange, now a picturesque link between the eastern and western shores, was a settlement of major importance in medieval days. Furness Abbey records of 1396 make reference to 'our grange in Borrowdale', the chief farm from which they managed their mountain estates.

Even the earliest of travellers, who gazed upon the high and

Bowder Stone

unknown mountains with considerable dread, were enticed
into Borrowdale just far enough to see the Bowder Stone,
poised, all 2,000 tons of it, below Grange Fell, and above the
Derwent. The grand inconsequence of the position of this tri-
angular mass of metamorphic rock, 36 ft. high, caused them to
speculate, as sightseer after sightseer still does, on how this ver-
itable giant of a rock, swept along by the force of the advan-
cing glacier, thus came to rest.

103

It was in this valley, in a cave on Castle Crag, that Cumberland-born Millican Dalton spent many contented years. He was, by all accounts, a lovable, intelligent man to whom the adventure of an open-air life was all important. He earned a small livelihood as a tent-maker and guide, sported a Tyrolean hat, rode a blue bicycle, and lived to be eighty.

From the water, continuing across Great Bay, all else is eclipsed by the grandeur of the mountains, Glaramara, Great End, Scafell and Scafell Pike, which compose the spectacular, rugged rockscape of Borrowdale; to many the epitome of the Lake District.

Leaving the head of the lake the launch turns to ply her way down beside the beautifully wooded western shore. A proposal of nineteenth-century industrialists to run a railway beside this shore, to ease the transport problem of the slate quarry at Honister, caused Rawnsley to exclaim: 'Let the slate trains once roar along the western side of Derwentwater, and Keswick as a resort of weary men in search of rest will cease to be.'

By 1923, when Hugh Walpole joined the local population, possible desecration by the railway was forgotten, and the problem of the car had hardly begun. Seeking serenity to write, he bought Brackenburn, a house with an enviable position at Manesty. Walpole's love of the Lakes was a genuine one, but his restless temperament did not allow him to be content at Brackenburn for any length of time. After spending a few weeks, or months beside Derwentwater, writing continuously, he would say *au revoir* to his study and depart to rejoin his friends and participate in the social life of London. His need for the metropolis satisfied, back he would come to write, drive through the valleys, take the ferry to Keswick, and periodically organise alterations to his house. The lake view, from the originally one-storeyed house, was slowly blurred by the growing trees; so Walpole added first one storey and then another.

Living at Brackenburn, the Lakeland scenes that he loved, the remote farms of Watendlath and Rosthwaite, wove themselves into a background for the tale of Judith Paris, and the family he named Herries. Walpole spent his last days at Brackenburn, and when he died, in 1941, he was buried in the church-yard of St. John's, Keswick.

Scafell and its companion peaks are now behind us. Catbells extends above the trees of Brandlehow; and, looking ahead, the prospect has changed to encompass the lesser height of Latrigg overlooked by Skiddaw. A cormorant flies overhead. Derwentwater will keep it amply supplied with fish. The excellence of the fishery from the birds' point of view, though the angler may not care for the competition, is confirmed by the presence of a heronry near the western shore. Herons are conservative birds; having once established a heronry, usually in the tree-tops, they return to it year after year. But although the blue-grey herons, long bills poised to spear their prey, may be seen in their habitual motionless stance beside any of the lakes and tarns, Derwentwater now has the only regular lakeside heronry in the Lake District.

Rampsholme was given to the Trust as a landing place for picnics, and the sanctified isle of St. Herbert has not altered its name since the priest retreated there well over a thousand years ago. It was in the year A.D.687 that St. Herbert, and his

Cottage at Brandlehow

friend, St. Cuthbert of Lindisfarne, died within an hour of each other, as if in answer to their prayer to depart from this earth and reach the gate of Heaven together. Long afterwards a ferry was employed in bringing pilgrims to the island. A smith at Portinscale made and sold images of the local saint. No doubt he found it a profitable livelihood. In 1374 Bishop Appleby instructed the Vicar of Crosthwaite, in whose parish Keswick then lay, to go to the island each year on St. Herbert's day, and celebrate mass. Following a long period of observance, the custom fell into disuse until the indefatigable Canon Rawnsley rallied his congregation and revived the pilgrimage for a few years.

Contemporary children and adults are familiar with the legendary isle in the guise of *Owl Island,* where Beatrix Potter's *Squirrel Nutkin* had his adventures. Red squirrels, and their association with the island is said to be based on fact, do build their dreys in the woods of nearby Brandlehow. These endearing creatures, with their beautiful bushy tails, have, as yet, not been dispossessed by their more destructive grey cousins from the south. Carefully protected in the Lake District, one of the few regions of England where red squirrels are still found, some of them, particularly at Brandlehow, have become surprisingly tame.

Hawse End, the stepping-off point for Catbells and Newlands, is the last stage before skirting Nichol End and Portinscale. It was about fifteen years after Mr. Harker of Lodore had introduced his tours of the lake by launch that the first motor-boat was seen and heard at the Nichol End ferry; a ferry which in all probability originated from the desire of medieval pilgrims to visit St. Herbert's Island. Introduced to Derwentwater by a ferryman named Dick Gill, it did not deter his grandfather, a great local character and a friend of Canon Rawnsley, from continuing to row passengers across, a service he was still performing at the age of eighty-four. The Gills had been connected with this pedestrian ferry to Keswick for several generations. When the last ferryman Gill retired there was a fear locally that it might fall into disuse. Portinscale, which it serves, was immensely relieved when the versatile Mr.

Newby, 'owner of a good bass voice', took it over. So it is Mr. Newby's boat we look for when we walk past the Derwentwater Sailing Club, and beneath the trees to the sheltered little beach at Nichol End. Other launches operate from this jetty, but it is Mr. Newby who upholds the long tradition of the ferry.

In Portinscale, at the foot of the lake, the Derwent renews its identity, merges with the Greta, helps to swell Bassenthwaite, and flows calmly on through Cockermouth to the sea. But the lovely old stone bridge which used to cross it at Portinscale was weakened by heavy storms and, to the sorrow of the village, deemed unsafe. An attempt to pin down the exact date of its removal led to a local divergence of opinion. It was possibly the year Jack T. went into hospital, but only if that was the year the twins were born to Mrs. S. If, on the other hand, poor old Jack T. was hospitalised the year before the twins were born, then when precisely did disaster strike the bridge? The answer remained unsolved. However, by a process of domestic elimination it was narrowed down to the early 1950s. A Bailey Bridge, allowing buses to cross, took its place for a number

Bridge at Portinscale

of years. This was superseded by the present suspension footbridge, painted green and more in keeping with suburbia than
the Lake District National Park.

On beyond the wooded isthmus, where the swimmers
gather, the launch has nearly completed its fifty minute journey. Now the far vista reveals Helvellyn ranging out along the
eastern sky-line. Away to the west are the less familiar fells of
Hindscarth and Robinson. Close at hand, the gentle curve of
Crow Park allows the sheep to graze down to the water's edge.
With a practised hand the boatman returns us to the Keswick
jetty. We disembark, and pause to look up the lake whose perfection, impossible to describe, has caught us in its spell.

It was at the boating place one morning when the sun was in
sole command of the sky, and with only the faintest whisper of
a breeze, we watched a bat fly briefly to land on the boat-house
roof. Had we not seen it land we might not have spotted it at
all while it basked, as we did, in the warmth of the sun. Oddly
enough, only on the shores of Derwentwater have I seen a bat
fly in full sunlight. On Friar's Crag, we once saw one make its
short flight from one tree trunk to another.

But on the days when even the fairest of lakes, dimmed by
mist and steady rain, is inhospitable, then the Lake District
towns acquire a new dimension. Keswick, an ancient market
town, grew up around the river Greta at the foot of Derwentwater. Geared, in common with all Lakes towns, to tourism, its annual inrush of visitors is augmented in July by the
Keswick Convention which celebrated its centenary in 1975.

Long before the word 'tourist' existed this Lakeland town
was invaded by outsiders. Difficult as it may be to imagine,
during the reign of Elizabeth I, Keswick was an active mining
centre. Under the patronage of the Queen, German miners
from Bavaria arrived in force to employ their expert knowledge in working the local mines along the Newlands Valley.
The town's reaction to this irruption of men, tough, noisy and
bent on locating 'a lucky strike' of lead, copper, silver, even
gold, was not entirely friendly. No objections to mining on the
grounds of scarring the natural landscape crossed the towns-
people's minds, but a surge of adverse feeling against strang-

ers, encroaching on their home ground, who might deprive them of a living, or of a choice of wives. Their fears were not completely unfounded, for the marriage rate between Germans and local girls was high in the first few years of their coming. Although the people of Keswick did not make them wholly welcome, and some of the miners retreated to the seclusion of Derwent Isle, the situation eased with time. A number stayed on, and became integrated into the community.

Pack-horses were kept busy transporting the minerals to the lake, where they were transferred to boats for their journey to Keswick. The lake was in constant use as a highway. When it froze—a more regular occurrence then than now—a form of sledge was used.

When, after a century or so, the minerals ran out, Keswick's prosperity waned. Prior to the advent of tourism, its income depended on the wool trade and pencil-making. Graphite, locally 'wadd', or 'black cawke', was reputedly an accidental discovery. Shepherds used it for marking sheep, and as a remedy for colic. Its full possibilities once realised, pencil-making has not looked back. The local supply of graphite ceased, but the industry still flourishes.

The streets of Keswick were not intended for the heavy traffic they now carry. The extensive parking area between the town and The Heads brought about a slight alleviation of the problem, but the centre of Keswick will not be comfortable until it has been elevated to the status of a pedestrian precinct. It is difficult, for instance, to appreciate fully the striking white Moot Hall in the Market Place. Known to have existed in 1571, it is one of the few remaining links with the mining period, when it was the Receiving House at which the copper received the Queen's Mark. Rebuilt later, incorporating Radcliffe relics, it displays upon its narrow tower one of the oldest of one-hand clocks. Inside are the literature, leaflets and photographs relating to its present function as an Information Centre.

These Centres, also located in Hawkshead, Bowness, Ambleside and Grasmere, and by the time this is in print, possibly elsewhere, are run under the auspices of the Lake District

Special Planning Board, the National Trust, and the English Lake Counties Tourist Board. They provide a service in the way of printed and illustrated material relating to all aspects of the Lake District. Each Centre is a miniature Brockhole. They receive around 320,000 visitors a year, who emerge equipped with details of planned walks, fishing licences, National Trust properties, natural history, mineralogy, Mountain Goat and coach tours, a time-table of the Sealink cruisers and so on. A plethora of informative car and armchair reading. Excellent it is too except, perhaps, for the inclusion of a picture of thatched Tudor cottages adorning the shores of Windermere, on the British Rail Sealink leaflet. One can only suppose this was due to an excess of enthusiasm on the part of the compiler!

The Mountain Goat is a comparatively recent innovation. This fleet of white minibuses gives an invaluable means of travelling through the Lake District, particularly as, due to their manoeuvrability, they are able to undertake routes outside the range of the ordinary bus.

Keswick, a town of little other architectural distinction, has Greta Hall, now part of Keswick School, to revive memories of its august company of literary lions. Coleridge moved to Keswick in 1800 to be near Wordsworth. He believed he would be able to work and live equably at Greta Hall. Frequently this immensely gifted man is dismissed arbitrarily as miserable, quarrelsome and a burden to his friends; but his life was too involved to be fairly summarised in a few sentences.

He and Robert Southey married two sisters. For Coleridge this was a gesture, part of an idealistic plan, rather than a marriage of love, and a mistake from which he never fully recovered. We only have to turn the pages of Dorothy's *Journal* to realise in what high esteem and great affection he was held by the Wordsworths in the early part of their friendship. At Greta Hall he found the winters terrifyingly cold; Wordsworth was only fairly close at hand, and it was a tedious walk to Grasmere. He was also frustrated by his love for Sara Hutchinson, whose sister, Mary, was to marry Wordsworth. Unable to work, feeling both guilty and ill, Coleridge resorted to laudanum, a remedy as usual then as aspirin is today. Unable to cope with his family responsibilities, he was fortunate in having the good-natured Southey as a friend.

The Southeys joined the Coleridges at Greta Hall and stayed there for the rest of their lives. Coleridge troubled about his wife, did try to accept the role of husband and father, but found it intolerable; and finally, leaving his family behind, he departed from the Lakes, and never returned. For the last eighteen years of his life he lived in London at the home of James Gillman, who gave Coleridge both friendship and medical help. This indecisive man, whose extraordinary eloquence held his listeners spellbound, was once more able to write, and became recognised as one of the foremost critics in the history of literature.

Mrs. Coleridge, eventually realising that their separation was wise, remained with the Southeys under the companionable roof of Greta Hall.

Southey, surrounded by his vast library, worked hard, was appointed Poet Laureate and took part in local life. When seen out walking he generally had a book under his arm. He walked for the necessary exercise, not, like Wordsworth, to compose his poetry in the open air. Although his work gives little clue to the splendour of his surroundings, he did love Lakeland, the walk to Watendlath, and the view from Applethwaite under Skiddaw, being especially dear to him.

Shelley came to Keswick and looked upon Derwentwater, 'smooth and dark as a plain of polished jet'. But the Romantic aura built up by the Lake Poets had its sceptics. 'They make such a spluttering about it,' complained Charles Lamb, 'and toss their splendid epithets about them.' So, unannounced, he arrived to judge for himself. Once there he was entranced by the lakes in their net of mountains, and was forced to admit there was such a thing as that which was called 'Romantic'. Skiddaw was a 'fine creature', indeed. But after all, he could not live on Skiddaw, and the prospect of not seeing Fleet Street from time to time, would have caused him, he said, 'to mope and pine away'.

By Greta Bridge, the School of Industrial Art, owing its

foundation to Ruskin and Rawnsley, today attracts scores of visitors. So does the town's Museum. It is situated on the edge of Fitz Park, near the redundant railway station, itself the present home of the most up-to-date computerised railway exhibition in the world.

No attempt has been made to up-date the display arrangements of the Museum. Casual, and pleasantly old-fashioned, it holds a store of local interest. Walkers come to contemplate the 12 x 9 ft. model of Lakeland constructed by Joseph Flintoft nearly a century and a half ago. And no one can deny the fascination of the unique Rock, Bell and Steel Band which Joseph Richardson took to entertain Queen Victoria. Now destined to silence, it comprises 60 stones, 60 steel bars and 40 bells. Richardson experimented with rock from varying parts of the Lakes, before deciding that stones from Skiddaw were the most 'musical'. Relics of the Radcliffes, including a high-backed carved chair from their abandoned island home, jostle for pride of place with mementoes of Otley, Southey, Walpole and Peter Crosthwaite, founder of the original Museum.

Keswick now has its own church of St. John; its triumphant spire is seen from nearly every angle of the town. To find the venerable church of Crosthwaite we must go north out of the town for about a mile to the spot where, in A.D. 553, St. Kentigern is believed to have planted his cross in the valley of the

Castlerigg Stone Circle

two lakes. Maybe his preaching gave rise to a tiny chapel of wattle and wood. We may only guess. So when, about a century later, the good St. Herbert came to live on his Derwentwater Isle, virtually in the 'desert' (his name for that wild and lonely region), he was aware of a small Christian community not so far away at Crosthwaite.

Certainly, by 1181 a 'new' church was built by Alice de Romili, and its foundations are incorporated in the building we see today. Southey was a regular member of the congregation for forty years. The other name happily and eternally linked with Crosthwaite is Rawnsley. His name is woven into the history not only of Keswick and Derwentwater, to which he devoted unceasing thought and energy, but of the Lake District as a whole.

Derwentwater, the centre of many a lake tour, over-shadows the larger, less sought after Bassenthwaite. Most northern of all the lakes, with the grand outpost of Skiddaw watching over its eastern margins, and Barf and Lord's Seat to the west, it has the distinction of being actually named Bassenthwaite Lake, the others being 'waters' or 'meres'. When and why the distinction came about is not clear. Until, in pre-historic times, deposits brought down by the Greta and the Newlands Beck formed a two-and-a-half-mile alluvial flat, only one lake filled the floor of this valley. The difference in level between the two lakes is approximately 20 ft. Thus, except after continuous rain when the flats are flooded, the Derwent moves lethargically between them.

In the vicinity of Bassenthwaite various indications of early settlers have been discovered. An Iron Age fort crowns Castle How, and on the plain of Elva, reached by a minor road west of Ouse Bridge, is a stone circle, believed to date back to 2000 B.C. Where there is a circle time-honoured tales turn to fairies, and this one has long been known as Elf How.

The most impressive and best known circle in the Lakes is, undoubtedly, Castlerigg. Situated on a high and lonely plateau to the east of Keswick, it consists of a circle of 38 stones, with an oblong of 10 stones inside. Formerly wrongly described as a Druids' Circle, it is now considered to have a pre-historic significance relating to a pagan rite of the Bronze Age, about 1400 B.C. Whether your interest is engrossed by prehistory or not, the Castlerigg Stone Circle is an impressive sight.

The stones stand, it seems, within the very centre of the mist-shrouded mountains, a monument to the men and women of whom we know little but that this was their meeting place.

To the young Ruskin, taken by his parents to see the Castlerigg stones, they conjured up a vision of a giant playing skittles, who

> ' ... leaving the place, ere his ball he could swing,
> Had left all his ninepins stuck up in a ring.'

Although the fourth largest of the lakes, little is heard of four-mile long Bassenthwaite. There is a local saying that when cloud and rain encompass the rest of the Lake District, the sun will shine on Bassenthwaite. Unfortunately, other local weather prophets upset that optimistic maxim by affirming that if only a single cloud persists it will cast its shadow over Bassenthwaite. Which does not help us much as a forecast, but at least suggests Bassenthwaite Lake is determined to be different!

A lake of sails and oars, motor power being prohibited, Bassenthwaite has the supreme advantage of quiet. It has become the yachtsman's lake. On a favourable day, with a favourable breeze, a fleet of sailing craft will be spread out across the water. The Bassenthwaite Sailing Club, in common with most of the Lakeland clubs, offers facilities to visitors to launch sailing dinghies from their site. Yachtsmen and boatmen, particularly those who launch their craft upon any of the lakes for the first time, should take good heed of local advice, and always keep in mind the danger of sudden squalls, to which these mountain-ringed waters are prone.

The northern end of the lake, its foot, sees most of the activity. Here, between April and October, racing takes place on Thursdays and Sundays. The main class adopted by the Bassenthwaite Club is the GP14, but all classes frequent this splendid sailing water.

Appropriately, the principal event of the Bassenthwaite

Ouse Bridge

season is the annual August sailing week, drawing contestants and spectators from far afield. Appropriately, because Bassenthwaite saw the first of all Lake District regattas. Obviously, a regatta publicising a 'horserace' as a major attraction would hardly appeal today, as it did to the crowds who gathered near Ouse Bridge in 1780. A number of horses were towed out on barges into the middle of the lake. The barges, which had been plugged, were then sunk. The first horse to swim ashore was the winner. Another 'sport' consisted of ducks being chased by water spaniels.

That was two centuries ago. At the present time there are more people carrying binoculars, to watch the ducks and birds for their own sake, than ever before. Ornithologically speaking, the lakes are of greatest interest between October and April. Then numerous waterfowl may fly to these lower levels, temporarily free of the tourist craft. Winter brings flocks of gulls to roost at the foot of Bassenthwaite. Tufted duck, conspicuous for their black and white plumage, pochard, whooper swan and geese are some of the regular winter visitors. Often, as elsewhere, it may be only the keen bird-watcher who spots them.

This northern water, undisturbed by the speed addicts, has a good reputation amongst fishermen, who find it offers a wealth of sport. Scarness and Broadness Bays to the east, and the wide bays at the head of the lake are well known to anglers, who find no lack of perch or pike for their supper. Though fishing for trout with a rod and line is popular, it is reckoned that sitting on a bank, or boulder, and angling for perch is the most common form of fishing in the Lakes. To leave a baited hook unattended is against the law.

A notable absentee from both Bassenthwaite and Derwentwater is the char. Whilst being of little interest to the angler, because they are exceedingly difficult to catch, the most out-of-the-ordinary fish present in both lakes is the vendace. Confining themselves to the deepest water, like the char, they refuse to take anything the angler offers. Very occasionally dead vendace are found on the shore. Like the char, the vendace reached those lakes where it is now present during the Ice Age, and there it has stayed. Ullswater and Haweswater are the only other English lakes the vendace inhabits, where, to confuse the unknowing, it is called skelly.

The A66 road from Keswick follows the line of Bassenthwaite's western shore. Moving below Thornthwaite Forest and Wythop Woods it is so definitely bound for Cockermouth that it has lost the constant affinity with the lake which beautifies the roads skirting Coniston and Derwentwater. The decision to reconstruct it, rather than divert the heavy traffic outside the National Park was a sad day for the Lake District.

We shall not choose to hasten along with the road. If we did, in no time at all we should be moving away out of the Lake District to the coast. Instead, Bassenthwaite may first be admired from afar by turning aside at Braithwaite to venture a short distance up the Whinlatter Pass—the easier of the two passes to the Buttermere Valley—where, before all else is screened by the Forestry firs, there is a panoramic view of the head of the lake. Barf, where the outstanding shape of a white rock caused it to be known as The Bishop, is equally renowned as a viewpoint.

Despite the busy road the western shore is more accessible than from the east, and the landing for the hire of boats is at Piel Wyke, beyond Wythop Woods. Until not so very long ago

Early Morning on Bassenthwaite

the Keswick to Cockermouth single track line ran almost the
length of Bassenthwaite, and trains once steamed along beside
the lake.

It is sometimes suggested Bassenthwaite inspired Tennyson
in the writing of *Morte d'Arthur.* All we know for sure is that
whilst staying at Mire House, the poet discussed it with his
host James Spedding, an authority on Bacon, in the elite company of Carlyle and Edward Fitzgerald.

Mire House is east of the lake, as is the old church of Bassenthwaite. It is worth a diversion to visit the church, with its
ancient dedication to St. Bega, for it stands serenely amidst
the meadows on the very margins of the lake.

On this side of the water, the road is the same A591, which
has passed Windermere's *Low Wood Hotel,* taken its non-
stop run round Grasmere and Rydal, kept pace with the private banks of Thirlmere, seen Keswick and travelled on below
Skiddaw. Now, though it hugs the line of the fell well to the
east of the broad valley, there are exceptionally lovely pros-
pects of the lake. The sight of the southern reaches flooded by
the golden light of the evening sun, just before it disappears
behind Thornthwaite, is dazzling and unforgettable.

6

BUTTERMERE AND THE WESTERN LAKES

No one ever tries to disguise the fact that Borrowdale holds a record for rain, and that Seathwaite is the wettest place in the country. Rain is one of the indisputable features of the Lakes. Though rarely, it seems, does it act as a deterrent. In high season there are moments when one wishes it did! Generally speaking it is people who do not know the Lakes who say, as Arnold Bennett did on hearing of Hugh Walpole's proposed home beside Derwentwater, 'You will get wet through'. And so you jolly well might, if you wander about unprepared for a sudden shower.

Nowhere, however, does the sky perform so quick a change. It may wear a frown so fearsome we feel the sun has abandoned us forever, leaving the fells permanently cloaked in grey, and the colour drained from the lakes. Then, almost as if our sigh was heard, the clouds are brushed aside with a rapid hand, and once again lake and fell reveal a more seductive face. They say you may see four seasons in a day, find rain in one valley and sun in the next. Or, in the words of the bard of Rydal, 'The rain here comes down heartily, but is often followed by brighter, clearer weather.'

The one thing to do about the temperamental nature of Lakeland weather is to be prepared. The experienced abide by common sense rules never take unnecessary risks, and are only too willing to listen to the knowledgeable resident's caution. The Mountain Rescue Teams and the Lake Wardens are called to the assistance of people who do incredibly silly things, which a few minutes spent seeking advice before setting out might have prevented. If there just doesn't happen to be a knowledgeable resident at hand, then there is certainly no scarcity of National Park Wardens and Information Centres.

Choosing one of the 'brighter, clearer' periods, let us now leave Borrowdale behind to travel over the Honister pass till Buttermere comes into view, calm, undisturbed, a dream of a lake. This was the route of the four-in-hands, which continued in the Lake District long after they had been ousted by the motor car elsewhere. Some were seen right up to the 1930s. Starting from Keswick the horses had to be in fine fettle to pull the carriages up the gruelling ascent. The coachman, an impressive figure in a white hat, would encourage the more active passengers to foot it up the steepest gradient. Taking a whole day for the 'Buttermere Round', the return journey encompassed the stiff rise of Newlands Hause, where the land falls dramatically away into the valley.

Following a pattern similar to the Vale of Keswick, Buttermere and Crummock Water were once undivided. Slowly, Sail Beck deposited loose debris on the intervening rock bar until two separate waters emerged. With the not far distant Loweswater, it is sometimes remarked that three lakes now occupy the floor of the Buttermere valley; in actual fact Loweswater lies in a lateral valley to the west. Anyone who cares to climb Fleetwith Pike will gain a splendid view of all three.

Tumbling down beside the pass is Gatesgarthdale Beck, delighting the eye, and absorbing a handful of nameless streams on its way. At Gatesgarth — and fleeting back in time, *Gatescartheved,* 'top of the road gap', was the medieval name for the Honister — the beck forsakes its lively antics to flow placidly through the flats. On entering Buttermere its collection of stones and silt is forcing out a new promontory into the lake; thus, imperceptibly, a shore line alters.

Buttermere's setting below wooded slopes, steep crags and waterfalls is superb. An air of singular repose is communicated by the unexpected group of Scots firs at its head. With perfect clarity every line of tree and fell, every wayward cloud, or hovering bird, reappears at our feet. To the west is High Stile, and down the side of Red Pike the white ribbon of Sour Milk Gill, not the only Lakeland beck so named, threads its

Head of Buttermere

way from Bleaberry Tarn to cascade into the lake's north-west corner. Nowhere in this valley are we far from the music of the falls.

Below the long line of the Buttermere Fells the road runs parallel with the eastern shore. A shore of bays and rounded headlands, where it is possible to set off, by way of a gate, or a ladder-stile bridging the dry walling, on a walk around the lake. This is one of the easiest of all round-the-lake walks. Partly because Buttermere's longer shore extends little over a mile, and partly because the paths are good, keeping to the shore all the way, except for a brief diversion by Gatesgarth Farm, and at the foot of the lake. The figures of hikers, small in the distance, are frequently seen strung along the shore below High Stile, or, more adventurously, climbing the Scarth Gap to Haystacks and its upland tarns, or following the track to find the River Liza and Ennerdale. From this valley only on foot is there access to Ennerdale; the motorist must make his lengthy way around the intervening screen of fells.

Gone are the days when the attire of country lovers was restricted to drab shades of fawn and green. They gained full marks for camouflage, but not for safety. Yellow and flame coloured waterproofs, or cagoules, are becoming accepted gear on the fells, and their visibility, which might well save a life in an emergency, is striking.

Buttermere and Crummock are content to share one village between them, situated at the foot of Newlands Hause. The Victorian-renewed church, looking rather lost beside the road, two inns, a few farms, and a handful of cottages form the nucleus of Buttermere village. Notwithstanding its popularity and the traffic it sees in high season, Buttermere has changed little over the years. I remember a day years ago when we had walked through Newlands from Hawse End on Derwentwater, how welcoming was, and still is, the simple little cafe attached to Croft Farm.

Facing you four square on arrival is the unassuming *Fish Hotel.* A recent landlord of the *Fish,* Nicolas Size, adopted writing as a second interest, and based one of his books, *Secret Valley,* on the Viking invasion of the Buttermere valley.

Behind the inn cars must come to a full stop. Indeed, as cars may be driven no further in this direction, a word on footwear might be timely. Undertaking even a relatively straightforward walk in the Lakes wearing unsuitable shoes is as foolish as attempting to climb Great Gable in sandals and jeans. From Buttermere, everyone, at some time or another is inclined, quite understandably, to set off for Scale Force. A delightful walk through woods and meadows, but with a reputation for being wet and slippery underfoot. We have met strangers who have had to turn back simply because their feet were clad in fashion shoes instead of boots, or at any rate strong, preferably waterproof, shoes.

Scale Force is discovered about a mile up Scale Beck. The changing tempo of a running stream taking a sudden leap over a wall of rock, to fall with glorious abandon into a pool below, is irresistible. And Scale, cascading over 125 ft., is one of the outstanding waterfalls of the National Park; notably when the rainfall has been obligingly heavy, preferably just prior to your visit.

121

Ducks at Buttermere

Unable wholly to repel the frown of Mellbreak, a hard mass of rock rising abruptly from the shore, Crummock is a curiously solemn lake. Let us have the unrelenting fell behind us, and stand upon Ling Crag, a rocky promontory at its foot. There is, I know nothing original in the suggestion. Ling Crag is Crummock's renowned viewpoint, looking across the surface of the lake to the oasis of Rannerdale, sheltering below the distinct peak of Whiteless Pike. Northwards, Grasmoor stretches its long back like a great creature at rest.

Crummock owes its unmusical name not, like Windermere, Coniston and so many of the lakes, to the Norse influence, but to the Britons, who called it *crumbo*, meaning 'crooked'. Though it is reasonable to suppose it was the valley itself they referred to as 'crooked'.

These being the English Lakes, the largest of which are comparatively small, Crummock, though only 3½ miles long, ranks as one of the larger waters. The valley road bounds its eastern shore, sometimes beside, sometimes, as round the rock of Hawse Point, above the lake. Apart from the headland of Rannerdale, the fells crowd in upon Crummock. Once there was a settlement in Rannerdale near the union of stream and lake. A tiny chapel was here, twin probably to the original one at Buttermere, 'the most diminutive of all in England'. Now, over two centuries have passed since dalesmen dwelt and farmed in Rannerdale; no signs are left to remind us of their isolated existence.

The Lake poets all knew this valley well. It was Southey who, when out in a boat on Crummock one day, enthusiastically declared, 'of all the scenes in the land of the Lakes, that from the middle of Crummock is assuredly the greatest'. He and his companions had walked over the wild mountain track from Ennerdale to arrive at an inn at the lake foot. There it was that they enquired about hiring a boat. But this lake, too, remote then to be prepared for visitors, was 'not supplied like Windermere and Keswick'. 'Never,' wrote Southey later, 'did adventurers in search of pleasure set forth in a more rotten and crazy embarkation — it was the ribs and skeleton of a boat; however there was no other.'

Today, Buttermere, Crummock and Loweswater are all protected by the Trust, who let out the boats, and the fishing. Contemporary tourists, better catered for than Southey and his friends, should enquire at Croft Farm in Buttermere village, or, for Loweswater and the northern end of Crummock, at the *Kirkstile Inn*. The absence of power-craft will please those who prefer to pull on the oars, or hoist a sail. Trout fishermen will find good sport in all three lakes.

Without preamble our theme returns to *the* fish of the Lakes, the char, which once promoted a small, but renowned, cottage industry. Absent from the wider, shallower Derwentwater and Bassenthwaite, the char reappears in the deeper waters of Buttermere, 94 ft., and Crummock, 144 ft. Migrating from northern seas to spawn, the char was landlocked, like the vendace, after the Ice Age. Unable to survive in a temperature exceeding 59°F it is only found in the deepest, coldest lakes. Thus an experiment to introduce it into the shallower water of Loweswater was quite unsuccessful.

Char resemble trout in appearance, but have more resplendent colouring. William Gilpin has left us a vivid description of eighteenth-century net fishing for char in Windermere. 'A parcel of char, just caught, and thrown together into the luggage-pool of a boat makes a pleasant harmony of colouring. The green olive-tint prevails; to which a spirit is here and there given by a light blush of vermilion. These pleasing colours are assisted by the bright silvery lights, which play over the whole; and which nothing reflects more beautifully than the scales of the fish.'

Once they had been netted, potting the char was a seasonal Lakeland occupation undertaken by the women. The fish, well seasoned with salt and pepper, mace, nutmeg and cloves were packed into a deep earthenware pot. Clarified butter was poured over them, and they were cooked slowly for about three hours. After draining, the char were extracted, the skin and bones removed and the fish transferred to small pots to be covered with more melted butter. The individual pots were then despatched far and wide, and local hotels advertised 'charrpot' as a delicacy of the house.

Since the cessation of netting, fishing for char has developed into a specialised art mostly practised by local people. The recognised method is trolling, 60 to 90 ft. down, in the deepest area of the lake and always with a shiny lure. Hence have arisen the tales of gold beaten down. Using a rowing boat the fisherman moves down the lake with rods on either side, and a line bearing a number of spinners and hooks. If a fish is hooked, and, naturally, the reason for all this is that char are difficult to catch, it jerks sufficiently to ring the bell attached to the end of the rod. The fisherman leaves his oars, which are not in rowlocks but on thole-pins, and hauls in his line.

It was, according to De Quincey's account, to witness or participate in the char-fishing that the notorious John Hatfield first came to Buttermere's *Fish Inn*.

The story of Hatfield revolves round Mary, the Beauty of Buttermere. Hatfield was an ambitious, unscrupulous nine-

Fish Hotel

teenth-century con-man born in Cheshire under the name of
Hope. He married the daughter of Lord Robert Manners, and
after spending the £1,500 he received as a wedding gift
deserted his wife and child. Bereft, his wife died not long afterwards, whilst he, pretending to be a relation of the Duke of
Rutland, ran into debt for which he was imprisoned. A gulli-
ble clergyman lent him money to repay his debts, but Hatfield
was quickly behind prison walls again. Without conscience,
this time he persuaded a girl living nearby to redeem him and,
once free, he married her. A brief interlude of domesticity in
Somerset was followed by further financial difficulties; then
again Hatfield left his wife and travelled north.

On arrival in Keswick, in 1802, the unrepentant adventurer
now claimed to be the Hon. John Hope, and a Member of Par-
liament. Riding to Buttermere he put up at the *Fish Inn,* then
only a cottage. He was waited upon by fair Mary Robinson,
daughter of the landlord, whom with little ado, he wooed and
wed, at Lorton church. A grand match it seemed for a country
lass. Disillusionment came speedily. Within a year justice

caught up with him and John Hatfield was tried, not for bigamy, but for forgery, and hanged. After the furore subsided, Mary settled back into local life, married a farmer from Caldbeck, and retired into happy obscurity.

All the Lake Poets took an equal share in broadcasting the story. Wordsworth, whose birthplace, Cockermouth, though divided by a distance of twelve miles, is Buttermere's most accessible town, regarded Mary with neighbourly concern. She was only two years younger than the poet;

> 'We were nursed, as almost might be
> On the same mountain . . . !

In fact the tale once publicised, sparked off a whole series of ballads and verse, including a melodrama which had a successful run at Sadlers Wells. To those familiar with the Lakes the rough translation of Buttermere, village and lake, to a stage set caused much amusement. Mary and Charles Lamb visited Sadlers Wells with Southey, and their impressions were conveyed to the Wordsworths in a letter from Mary: 'We had prodigious views of her (Mary Robinson) father's house in the vale of Buttermere—mountains very large like haycocks and a lake like nothing at all. If you had been with us you would have laughed the whole time . . . . ' Would William have laughed? I wonder.

Another legendary character of the Buttermere valley is 'Wonderful Walker'. A name featuring in every Lakes guide since Wordsworth first eulogised his virtues. Born in Seathwaite, the son of a yeoman, he came to be school-master at Loweswater, and later, both schoolmaster and curate of Buttermere. Robert Walker, an early advocate of time and motion study, believed no moments should be lost which might be put to some practical purpose. His parish was so tiny it entitled him to a minimal stipend. His annual income never exceeded £50. To provide for his wife and twelve children he sought other sources of income, working a smallholding, brewing ale. One of his innovations was fishing by draught-net in Crummock. For this he received a half-penny for each cast made. On leaving Buttermere he took up a curacy at Sea-

Carling Knott, Loweswater

thwaite. His parishioners always thought well of him for living as they did, working with them and for them. He strove to educate his children, and when he died in 1802 at the age of ninety-three, his legacy to them was, incredibly, £2,000.

Walker's life exemplifies the spartan existence to which numerous rustic clergy of the more isolated Lakeland valleys were accustomed at that period.

In this trinity of lakes Little Loweswater deserves to be appreciated for itself alone, rather than as an afterthought to the Buttermere round. From the centre of the Lake District I prefer to approach it over Whinlatter Pass with its superlative backward picture of Bassenthwaite Lake. Gradually, the Forestry Commission's unrelenting rows of fast-growing conifers give way to the treeless slopes of Lorton Fell. Turning south at the foot of the pass the flowery pastures of Lorton Vale, beloved by Wordsworth, tempt us to meander. But we will go on down Scale Hill, by the splendidly-situated old coaching inn, now a hotel, through the village, and on to Loweswater lake. Staying close to the north-eastern shore the road, not intended for heavy traffic, goes on, though we shall not go with it, to meet the Cockermouth road.

Sheltering below the decided rise of Carling Knott and hidden from Crummock by the bulk of Mellbreak, Loweswater is remotely situated at the top of the short valley. We have arrived at its foot, where Park Beck slips away on its short journey to Crummock, which has the River Cocker to carry off its own surplus. Now, digressing briefly, to follow the Cocker as it pursues its winding and lovely way through Lorton Vale, we discover it enveloped by the Derwent at Cockermouth. Moreover, the Derwent, having already contributed to Derwentwater and Bassenthwaite, thus acquires connections with five of the major lakes before it reaches the sea.

Loweswater is one of the less-frequented lakes. The coach on its lakes tour, the car laden with the latest design in transportable craft, prefer to dally by longer and more accessible shores. The angler and the walker take quiet pleasure in its serenity. There is no island to break the surface of the lake the Norsemen called 'leafy water'. The reeds, the water-lilies, reveal that, although more or less equalling Buttermere in size, it is much less deep. Nowhere does its depth exceed 53 ft. Close to the pastures at the lake foot, cattle, as unheeding of us as the ubiquitous sheep, ruminate in the shallows. Seemingly, they are always there.

As the sun and clouds play perpetual games of hide and seek across the faces of the fells, and the spread wings of a solitary gull are mirrored in the 'bosom of the lake', it is pleasant just to stroll along the tree-edged shore, stooping now and again perhaps, to examine the pebbles; their colours, no two the same, rose and brown and grey, fading as they dry. Some, re-washed by the briefest stirring of the lake, respond to the sun, and, sparkling, once more resemble semi-precious stones.

Exploring the lakes, it is not unusual to meet parties of youthful volunteers, schoolchildren, army cadets, Outward Bound groups, making an enthusiastic contribution to the necessary work of the Trust within the National Park. The clearing of timber in Holme Wood, the pretty wood decorating Loweswater at the base of Carling Knott, the construction of plank bridges at Blea Tarn and Tarn Hows, transporting wood for stile-making, are all projects in which they have played their part. On the southern bank of Loweswater is one of the adventure huts converted for the accommodation of such volunteers.

The highlight of the year in this valley is the Loweswater Show, generally held in September. Then the hills resound with the baying of hounds, and the excited cries of their owners, calling them as they approach the winning line. Hound trailing, a traditional Lakeland sport, is one of the outstanding events of the show. The dogs, in the prime of condition, sleek coated, lean limbed, bound over field and fell, scrambling under the fences, leaping the stone walls, for a distance of between five and ten miles, to follow a trail laid by two men who have, just previously, dragged round a length of hemp sacking soaked in aniseed. Each hound's reward is a dish of his favourite food, and the pride and affection of his master. The owner of the winning dog may take home a prize of about £10, or more, if he's a betting man and backed his dog to win.

The people who gather each year in the meadows of Loweswater are the men and women of Lakeland. This is a true country show, paying tribute to the way of life, both at work and at leisure, of those to whom the Lake District is home.

If Loweswater is remote, Ennerdale is even more so. In all probability it is the least visited of all the lakes. This is mainly due to its inaccessibility by road. Motorists searching for

129

Ennerdale continue out of the Loweswater valley, through Lamplugh and Roughton on a sharply twisting, switchback road, a road in harmony with its surroundings, not too narrow, but not wide. Even before the blossoming of the wild roses and the honeysuckle, its hedgerows are bright with a multitude of the white stars of the stitchwort, the earth-bound Star of Bethlehem. On arrival at Bowness it peters out altogether. A Forestry track continues up the valley, leading walkers only, for Ennerdale is their preserve, into the presence of some of the wildest, most rugged mountains of the Lake District.

Pale larch hem the base of Bowness Knott, and silver and grey beneath the jutting outline of Angler's Crag is the lake of Ennerdale. In 1973 the Trust, owner of most of the dale's few farms, purchased 234 acres of the south-west shore, including Angler's Crag, together with the 200-acre farm at Brimmer Head in Easedale. This brought the total area of the Lake District in their care to 90,000 acres. Rawnsley would have been proud indeed!

For Ennerdale, the most westerly of the lakes, holds a special place in the hearts of those to whom the Lake District is most dear. Did not Wordsworth link his name with this 'haunt of cormorant and the sea-mew's clang'? Or in the words of a less renowned poet:

> 'The place is very still and lone,
> A wilderness of grass and stone
> Save where the sweet lake fills the Vale,
> And mirrors all the silent scene,
> Great mountain masses intervene
> Betwixt the world and Ennerdale.'

Since Annie Armitt of Rydal expressed her love for this valley in those words, the Forestry Commission has, of course, mantled the dale-head and the banks of the Liza with its all-embracing plantations.

The lower basin of the lake, from whence the River Ehen makes its exit, broadens out like a lop-sided mushroom to extend for about a mile from shore to shore. From the lake foot, because Bowness Knott and Angler's Crag push forward as if to half-enclose this uncharacteristic bay, it seems as if Pillar and Steeple, two giants of ice-chiselled rock, command the top of Ennerdale. Whereas, at the valley head, Great Gable reigns supreme.

From the southern shore, and to walk all around the lake is a strenuous eight miles at least, is seen the magnificent wall of the Red Pike range dividing Ennerdale from Buttermere.

The only signs of habitation, for man was slow to penetrate this isolated valley, are to the north, where there are the scattered farms of Mireside, Beckfoot, Howside, and How Hall. The last shows a nineteenth-century face to the world, but has foundations of a much earlier dwelling.

Tussocky mounds and hillocks divide us from the lake. Grass on stone and stone on grass. Here and there, almost as if to dispel the sense of solitude we've come to seek, a rustic bench and table beckons the holidaymaker to take his picnic, with supreme lake views to restore the careworn and the weary. Across the water on Crag Fell a line of dry walling comes into focus, stimulating admiration for the men who built it straight up the green-brown mountain, using the superabundance of stones to mark out their boundaries.

Edging the water are great bare boulders, huge chunks of

Picnic Place beside Ennerdale

rock, sun-warmed if the day has been well chosen. Sprouting intermittently between them, as if by accident, grows a holly bush or a shining clump of gorse.

Measuring the lakes in the dull order of size places Ennerdale, 2½ miles long and 1 mile wide across the northern bay, as number nine. If, on the other hand, we consult Professor Pearsall's table in which he arranged them according to their productivity, with southern Esthwaite as the most productive, then Ennerdale shares with Wastwater the title of the most 'primitive', or least productive. This lake basin, cut by the ice out of hard volcanic rock, in wild, desolate country, with the minimum of farming and habitation by its shores, harbours water which has scarcely altered since its birth.

When, in 1848, the coastal town of Whitehaven needed to improve its water supply, a man named Thomas Hawksley was sent to investigate the possibility of using Ennerdale as a fresh source. He was 'astonished' by the purity of its water, 'as soft as rainwater, as tasteful as spring water'. Unobtrusively, and with little fuss, the lake has been supplying Whitehaven with water ever since.

Fishing is restricted to the members of the Ennerdale Lake Fisheries Association, the umbrella under which the local angling clubs have been gathered. They are allowed a limited number of boats, or may fish from the shore, other than on either side of the Water Board's Intake House. This does not, however, restrict visitors from applying for permits. Swimming, by the human species that is, is not allowed in Ennerdale.

For the wild life of the Lake District, the essentially pure unproductive water of Ennerdale, lacking the seclusion of wooded islands, the protective screening of reeds and rushes, makes it an inhospitable lake. Even the solitary isle of stones below Angler's Crag may appear bare of life at a first glance. Invariably, a second look at the rocky pile will discern the long black outline of a cormorant or two using it as a watching-post. The fish-eating cormorant is not disturbed by the absence of cover, for like the plump dipper, the other regular bird of Ennerdale, it has the ability to swim under water. Unfortunately, the cormorant live in Ennerdale mainly on an exclusive diet of trout and char, for the lake has no other size-able fish.

One of the few inhabitants of the lake is a rare crustacean, *Mysis relucta,* which for want of a better name, and because, though smaller, it resembles the marine shrimp we all know, is called a freshwater shrimp. This small creature retires to the lake bottom by day, a long way down, for Ennerdale reaches depths of 148 ft., and rises to feed by night. As far as is known, it occurs in no other English lake. One theory for its arrival is that it owes its origins to a marine species forced inland during the later Ice Age. When the ice retreated, it was left isolated in the rock basin.

The biological study of the Lakes continues. Windermere, host to the freshwater biologists, has received the major part of their attention. In consequence it is the most studied lake in the world. Ennerdale's secrets have not yet been fully fathomed.

Wastwater, easily reached from the west coast, is cut off from the heart of Lakeland by a massive barrier of rock. The most direct gateway is through the passes of Wrynose and Hardknott. Needing a steady eye on the road, and a ready hand on the gears, they will not be the first choice of the inexperienced motorist. But once over the Wrynose you are brought down to the lovely Cockley Beck, where the valley, the charming valley of Wordsworth's Duddon will take you, if you wish, to Wastwater by a rather longer route.

However, we, having paused to listen to the bubbling music of the beck, will cross the bridge, open and close the gate, and brace ourselves for the Hardknott. With gradients of 1 in 3, and hairpin, often hair-raising, bends, the Hardknott should be treated with respect. These passes abide by the twisting route carved out by the Romans for their legions nearly 2,000 years ago. On a high strategic spur of Hardknott, beyond the crest, they built a fort: its relics remain not far from the roadway, where we look down over the long lakeless valley of Eskdale towards the Irish Sea. Then on through lovely Eskdale, past the *Woolpack,* a favourite inn, and Dalegarth, the brightly-painted station near to Boot.

'Ratty'

Affectionately known as 'Ratty', the single track train rattles over the rails, puffing merrily, thrilling for the young, nostalgic for the not-so, patronised by all. Origins are easily forgotten. This line was primarily for transportation of minerals from the Nab Gill mine to the estuary at Ravenglass. In 1912 this traffic ceased. Later a new 15-inch track was laid, and the 7-mile narrow gauge railway, Dalegarth to Ravenglass, blossomed into one of the foremost tourist attractions of the Lake District.

Much as we might wish to turn aside to see the fine waterfalls of Dalegarth, and of the Birker Beck, to walk to Eel Tarn or Devoke Water, or wander over through bracken and heather well off the recognised tourist track, Wastwater is our present goal.

My very first sight of Wastwater was from Great Gable. The beck was a spiral of white, vanishing into the lake. Distance diminished the renowned impact of the Screes, and the pale lake swept round seeming to merge with the flat land, beyond

Wasdale, fanning out to the sea. But in this book we are con-
centrating on the valleys, not scaling the heights for aerial
views, panoramic as we know them to be. So we will round
Irton Fell by way of Santon Bridge and Strands to see, beyond
the trees which guard the lake foot, a sudden and breathtaking
view of the incomparable Wastwater. Preferably on a day
when the sun dispels the clouds, for on such a day the play of
light and shade over the fantastic Screes reveals their incredi-
ble variation in colour; black gives way to brown, to red, blue,
green. From the crags of Ilgill Head they spill down almost the
entire length of the far shore, a spectacular precipitous drop of
over 1,000 ft. And, lost from sight, down they go, for a further
200 ft. below the water. From the unique curtain of shattered

The Screes, Wastwater

rock the eye is drawn to the perfect symmetry of the purple mountains at the lake head, which have been adopted as the emblem of the National Park. Midsummer it may be, but in all probability they have not cast off their more obstinate patches of snow. Yewbarrow is there, its craggy form hiding the shape of Kirk Fell. Scafell Pike peers above Lingmell. Great Gable, triumphant at the head, is the climax of this noble group, which cast their image into a lake of a brilliant Mediterranean hue.

Faithfully, the road keeps pace with each indentation of the western shore, forging out its path between the boulders and the hillocks, and over the incoming becks, to link the scattering of dwellings at Wasdale Head with the world outside the dale.

Wasdale is the territory of the climbing fraternity who, by tradition, foregather at the *Wastwater Inn,* hotel as it is now. This was the home ground of the celebrated innkeeper, Will Ritson. Contemporary with Wordsworth and Professor Wilson, Ritson, a born raconteur, entertained the company at the *Wastwater Inn* with highly exaggerated tales. His reputation for tall stories led to the local saying that Wasdale had the highest mountain, deepest lake, smallest church, and biggest liar in all England. As the first licensee he was landlord till 1879, lived on till he was eighty-three, and died at Strands. His name is perpetuated in the little waterfall above the inn, christened Ritson Force.

Across a couple of fields is the diminutive church, a church still lit by the soft glow of oil lamps, and secluded, almost from sight, by its protective yews. Here are remembered, with moving simplicity, the men who lost their lives amongst the mountains they loved.

Looking up to the dalehead, the close patterning of the numerous stone walls resembles, from a distance, a rudimentary fortification. With their profusion of stone the people of the Lake District have never lacked material for building. On the contrary, it is said the thickness of the walls on some of the oldest cottages was not, principally, to preclude a howling draught, but to use up the multiplicity of stones. Sometimes

Wasdale Head

after very heavy rain there is, as it were, an additional delivery from fell to vale. As on the day in 1938 when the rain, 9 inches in 36 hours, was exceptional even for the Lake District. The Lingmell Beck, born on the side of the mountain of the same name, swelled into a raging torrent. The force of the water scouring the mountain sides, loosened and brought down with it a multitude of stone and small rocks, covering two of the fields of Wasdale to a depth of a foot or more.

137

These two western lakes, Ennerdale and Wastwater, were rarely included in the itinerary of the first visitors to Lakeland. Not that inaccessibility ever deterred Wordsworth and his friends. In the summer of 1809 a party of anglers spent a week in the environs of Wastwater. Led by Wilson of Elleray, it included both Wordsworth and De Quincey. Journeying through Eskdale to Wasdale they were accompanied by a dozen ponies carrying the camping requisites for the expedition. In the presence of the primitive beauty of Wasdale, fishing, for the lake is rich in game fish, was interspersed with high thinking.

Nevertheless the isolation of Wastwater, emphasised by its rugged environment of bare rock and scree, was such that early cartographers had seen no reason to depict it on their maps. Similarly, as it was considered to be wrapped in gloom,

Wastwater dominated by Yewbarrow, Great Gabel & Lingmell

and highly inaccessible, some guide books did not bother to mention it. Those who did venture to its remote dale, speculated that the 3-mile long lake, which had never been known to freeze over, might be bottomless. It was Jonathan Otley who first estimated that it must be at least below sea level.

Men left England and travelled far afield, crossing oceans to trace the source of the Nile, or explore the deserts of Australia; but it was not until 1893, less than a hundred years ago, that Hugh Robert Mill, following Otley's initial findings, set about a detailed investigation of the English lakes. He surveyed each one from a rowing boat, taking soundings with a lead line. Mill procured the first true picture of the lake bed of each and every lake. The contour lines on the current Ordnance Survey Maps are based on his depth findings. Mill confirmed Otley's assumption that the glacier had cut so deeply into this valley, that Wastwater, having a maximum depth of 258 ft., is below sea level in places.

Also known to all who love the wild solitudes of Wastwater is that it is a lake of extreme moods. No other lake imparts, with such intensity, the contrast between sun and storm. On a day of threatening skies, when the majestic peaks are beheaded by cloud and mist, the squally wind cold, then Wastwater, its remarkable Screes turned sinister, is black and forbidding, calling forth echoes of bygone fears. Echoes quickly dispelled as the trepidation of mere man is stilled in admiration of the divine austerity of Wastwater.

7

THIRLMERE TO ULLSWATER

For many decades now the natural inclination has been to hurry past Thirlmere. Prohibitive notices, alien to the spirit of the Lake District, were its only greeting. Thirlmere was a lake that had been loved and lost, sacrificed to the thirst of Manchester. The desolate change brought to the lake by the decision to use it as Manchester's tap had shocked all Lakeland lovers. Protests were loud, but not effective enough to halt the desecration of the landscape, a landscape which had moved Gray to write of 'the little shining torrents' which hurried down the rocks to the lake, 'with not a bush to overshadow them, or cover their march, all is rock and loose stone up to the very brow'. Some sixty years later a merry group, including the families of both Wordsworth and Southey gathered round 'a gypsy fire' under Raven Crag enjoying one of their innumerable picnics. Formerly, variously known as Wytheburn Water and Leathes Water, the lake was crossed in the middle by a primitive wooden bridge on stone piers. Some writers referred to it as two lakes. In its new form as a reservoir it was lengthened towards Dunmail Raise, and the water level was raised by 54 ft. Consequently, the main coaching road between Ambleside and Keswick had to be diverted. The Wordsworths' painstakingly inscribed Rock of Names was blown up, the fragments gathered together again and re-sited.

Ever since this unprecedented decision by Manchester to purchase the whole of the Thirlmere valley watershed, preservationists have exemplified it as a blatant act of spoilation. It was regarded as a warning signal of previously undreamt of dangers to the environment.

Thirlmere

Meanwhile, the Mancunians congratulated themselves on the acquisition of an excellent additional water supply, and a triumph of engineering. Generally speaking the higher the lake, and the more it is enclosed by barren rock and crag, the purer the water. The naturalist may sigh because it is unproductive, but the waterworks engineer lets forth a silent cry of thanksgiving: he knows it is ideally suited for human use. Thirlmere then, a deep 3-mile water below Helvellyn, both in a valley 533 ft. above sea level and subject to heavy rainfall, was the perfect solution to Manchester's problem. Ten years were spent in constructing the dam, and the 96-mile aqueduct conveying the water to a continually expanding city. It was in 1894 that the first Thirlmere water gushed into Manchester.

After so long there is little point in rushing by Thirlmere, still influenced by the spirit of indignation which germinated over eighty years ago. For to us, who never knew it in its natural form, Thirlmere, undisturbed by human activity, has a withdrawn appeal of its own.

Once acquired for the value of its water, the lake was bound to be enclosed to protect it from impurities. The closely packed afforestation took place between 1910 and 1925 as a means of preventing soil erosion, and the continual fall of stones and silt into the lake. Approximately 2,000 acres of the lower slopes were planted. The fast-growing firs, producing timber, were basically an economic venture. Quickly, the bare crags were unbecomingly draped in formal lines of dark, and unprepossessing fir. Nature abhors straight lines, it is reassuring that in present and all future plantations within the National Park, economy is being blended with the art of landscaping.

Yet the much criticised acres of fir, proving to be not quite as lifeless as they seemed at first, have given sanctuary to some of the native fauna. Deer roam Thirlmere, including about fifty red deer which have strayed from the deer forest of Martindale. Red squirrels will live contentedly among the Norway spruce, and nest-boxes attract tit-mice and pied fly-catchers to breed. And, since the 1960s two forest trails have been opened up to encourage our interest in the valley. One is from The Swirls, above the eastern shore, where the Helvellyn Gill dances down the mountain side. The other, beside Launchy Ghyll across the water, climbs up just 300 ft. Visitors are not expected to skip up it with the agility of the native sheep, but, says the Waterworks leaflet, 'with perseverance'. You'll find the leaflet in a neat box at the foot of the trail.

From the west of lake road the cry of geese may be heard, the murmur of a waterfall, or, indeed, for we must be realistic, the whirr of a power-driven saw. There are glimpses of the lake, and, from Bull Crag, an uninterrupted view. There may be walkers descending the tracks over the Armboth Fells from Watendlath. One thing is certain, the road is decidely bumpy, encouraging us to linger, rather than take it at speed. Near to its meeting with the A591 at the head of the lake, the low white solitary building of Wythburn church, which escaped the flooding of the valley, marks the beginning of the easy track up Helvellyn. At the foot, under Raven Crag, the road crosses the dam and moves on to the unrestrained and pastoral beauty of St. John's in the Vale.

Launchy Ghyll

No immediate plans are in the offing for further access to Thirlmere, but the Waterworks authorities and the Lake District Special Planning Board are working out a scheme to extend access to Haweswater, Manchester's second reservoir. Haweswater, 200 ft. deep, and 694 ft. above sea level, even higher than Thirlmere, is the furthest east of all the lakes. Probably its isolated position accounted for the fact that its conversion caused rather less protest. It goes without saying that the residents of Mardale felt the disappearance of the village as a deep personal loss. I quote the vivid recollection of Handley Laycock, a visiting fell-walker in the 1930s, when initial work on the reservoir had just commenced. He had walked from Brotherswater, over the Nan Bield Pass and down to Haweswater:

> *'I put up at a farm in the old hamlet (Mardale) by the lake, and had a good supper, bed and breakfast for 3/-! The farmer's wife told me how sad they all were at having to leave their ancestral home because Haweswater was soon to be greatly enlarged by a new dam so that its water could be piped to Manchester, and this hamlet with its church and everything would be at the bottom of the lake.'*

Tree-felling, Thirlmere Forest

As is all too evident, that is exactly what happened. Four farms, the church and the *Dun Bull Inn* were submerged and lost for ever, though part of the stonework of the old church was incorporated into the new dam. Readers who delight in statistics may care to learn that this unique dam is 1550 ft. long, 120 ft. high, and the concrete required to complete it measured 140,000 cubic yards. There are 44 independent buttresses, each 35 ft. wide. The lake level was raised 95 ft. and the reservoir now has a water capacity of 18,662 million gallons. Not till 1940 did Manchester receive its intitial supply from Haweswater by means of a 9-mile tunnel through Mardale, down the Longsleddale valley to Garnett Bridge, near Kendal, from whence it is conveyed to link with the Thirlmere aqueduct.

The wild regions of Haweswater and Mardale have been harnessed to the human need for priceless water, but the rigid landscaping of Thirlmere was not repeated. Slim belts of fir hold the shore at intervals. We miss the natural indentation, and the inconsequential arrival of the streams, for now the fells below High Street plunge steeply into the artificial level. A 2½-mile lake has become a 4-mile reservoir. From Bampton, where the Haweswater Beck joins the River Lowther, we may drive its length. The walker might as well save his legs for less circumscribed ground. Passing the only domestic building of the dale, the *Haweswater Hotel,* which took over the licence of the *Dun Bull,* the road keeps pace with the eastern shore. The massive dam and the solitary twin arches of the castellated straining wall are there to be admired, but the lake from here is out of bounds, though not out of sight.

The Haweswater's expected trout and perch are joined by both a smaller version of the Windermere char, known as Lonsdale char, and skelly, a variety of the whitefish known to Derwentwater and Bassenthwaite as vendace. However, the angler will see little of any of them, for fishing, as in Thirlmere, is strictly limited, and permission has to be obtained from Manchester.

Travelling the shore road is an opportune place in which to revive memories of days long past. This was the land of Hugh

Holme, first 'King of Mardale', a refugee from the south after his implication in a plot against King John. A cave in the isolation of Riggindale served as his first home. Panic over, it was safe to return, but he chose to stay in the Lakes—as have so many since—and founded a connection with the valley which lasted 700 years.

Near the foot of the lake, Thornthwaite Hall, a fine Elizabethan house, was once owned by the Curwens. Although, apart from a reference to Haweswater, little real identification appears in the book, Anthony Trollope is believed to have used it as the setting for *Can You Forgive Her*, the first of the Palliser novels.

Bordering the eastern shore Naddle Forest harbours relics of primeval woodland, and on Wallow Crag eagles, which forsook the Lakes a century and a half ago, established a regular nesting place.

Climbing out of Haweswater, up to Mardale Common through Swindale, Tailbert and Keld the track is known as the Old Corpse Road. It dates back to the time when, in valleys as thinly populated as Mardale, burial grounds were few and far between. Corpses had to be conveyed long distances, in this instance all the way to the parish church at Shap. These arduous journeys, complemented by tales of ghosts and supernatural incidents, only ceased in the eighteenth century when a graveyard was added to Mardale chapel.

Now we have arrived at the head of the lake, where The

Haweswater Dam

Rigg thrusts out like an arm, its hand gloved in evergreen. Seeing the mirrored image of Harter Fell, and the flat, marshy
grassland running up the dale, we may almost forget the flooding of the valley. Motorised transport has to be abandoned,
for the unfrequented tracks out of the Haweswater valley
beckon only those who are stout of heart and boot. The pass of
Nan Bield leads to Kentmere, with its memories of the Gilpins
and a lake drained over a century ago. On the lake bed were
found spearheads used by the Norsemen, and an oak dugout
canoe. Long Sleddale is reached over the Gatescarth Pass, and
tracks go west over the fells which culminate in the great
Roman road of High Street.

We leave Haweswater, knowing there is regret for its lost
freedom, but if there had to be a reservoir, then rather this eastern water on the outskirts of Lakeland than any other. And
now from the two reservoirs let us turn to the two lakes found
between them.

Lying like a grey and silent pool at the foot of the Kirkstone
Pass is Brotherswater. A riot of becks stream down the rock-
strewn mountainsides to unite, and be engulfed by the waiting
lake. Hemmed in by lofty mountains vanishing into the
clouds, the Kirkstone wears an aspect of stern solemnity. The
long descent snakes down between crags, hefty shoulders of
rock, and the shelving screes of Caudle Moor. At its foot are
the flat green enclosures heralding Brotherswater, and its
wooded western shore.

The smallest of the lakes, its total length of half a mile hardly exceeds the widest distance between its banks. Formerly
known as Broadwater, the change to Brotherswater reputedly
took place after the tragic drowning of two brothers who fell
through the ice. Along with Hartsop Hall, the lonely farmhouse at the foot of Dovedale, and a generous acreage of surrounding fell land, it is a further lake owned by the Trust.
Small craft may be privately launched, but there are no boats
for hire. As to fishing all I have ever learnt is that it is free, the
trout small and the perch evasive. On the other hand there is a
saying that there are always fish for 'them that knows how to
take them'.

147

Quite lately we walked the track past the *Brotherswater Inn,* below High Hartsop Dodd, and, saving for another day the left turn into Dovedale, skirted the Hartsop woods to meet the lake's western shore. There we paid silent tribute to the solemn grandeur of the scenic picture across the water, dominated by the insistent height of Middle Dodd, just west of the pass.

We went through the gate, over the modest bridge, and on to Low Hartsop, the hamlet sheltering between Lingy Crag and Low Hartsop Dodd. Incidentally, I discovered that the residents to whom we spoke were as little able as I to immediately identify all the fells in the vicinity bearing the suffix, Dodd. 'Dodd' alone is no other than the medieval name for a rounded hill.

Low Hartsop was once a thriving community dependent on the woollen industry for its livelihood. Today, it is a picturesque hamlet with a collection of sixteenth- and seventeenth-century cottages clustered about Pasture Beck. One or two still have the spinning galleries where women, born to a life of hard work and thrift, sat and spun, using all the available hours of daylight.

Tempting as it is to continue out of Low Hartsop and stroll beside the pellucid waters of the Hayeswater Gill, we will turn back, for we have another goal in view.

Brotherswater is, to the motorised tourist, often no more than a lonely mere glimpsed *en route* to the more expansive glories of Ullswater. Yet, spectacular as the route over the Kirkstone to Patterdale may be, for an unequalled first impression of Ullswater it is best approached from the north on the A5091. Lonely Troutbeck, and the bleak moors of Matterdale, are left behind. Decreasing speed as the road narrows through Dockray, we wind downhill between the parks of Gowbarrow and Glencoyne. The road curves and, almost without introduction, the mountains, seeming to tower straight up from the shore, and again straight down into the deep recesses of the lake, are suddenly revealed in their full mysterious majesty. When I first came this way, it was one January day, the silent mountains wore a raiment of snow, the lake was a heavenly blue, the trees stood silhouetted against the sky, (yes,

Ullswater from Gowbarrow

they were picture-postcard colours) and I realised why Ullswater, once seen, is never forgotten.

Approaching from this direction we have arrived at the western shore. The pretty road, travelling in obedience to the margins of the lake, divides, going north to Pooley Bridge, south to Glenridding. But first there is Aira Force to be seen, and Lyulph's Tower, both Trust protected, as is much of this end of Ullswater. The long lake is fed by a multitude of rivulets. Brotherswater, Angle Tarn and Hayeswater all despatch their becks to unite and speed lakewards through Patterdale. Others escape from mighty Helvellyn. But none arrives with more dramatic effect than Aira Beck.

The climb up the beck is escorted by the trees of Gowbarrow. Trees planted, not for timber, but purely for their scenic value. Intended to enhance the Romantic aura, which they certainly do, they have endowed Gowbarrow and Glencoyne, once medieval deer parks, with a rare beauty. Mountain ash, wild cherry, silver birch accompany oak and chestnut, broad-leaved, familiar. The Scots fir, its straight red trunk so sparsely clad, is host to Chile pine and other of its more exotic

149

Aira Force

Dacre Castle

cousins. All these and more, attend our climb to see the force dash with such vivacity over 65 ft. of rock.

The Duke of Norfolk's castellated folly, Lyulph's Tower, also owes its existence to eighteenth-century Romanticism. Nevertheless, it is believed to occupy the site of an ancient pele tower, others of which do still exist in the Lake District. Just north of Pooley Bridge, the village of Dacre has an outstanding example.

These defensive towers were built, mostly between the fourteenth and fifteenth centuries to withstand attack from invading forces, or raiding cattle thieves. Rising up in three storeys, they were built of the ubiquitous stone as a strong refuge into which a small settlement would retreat for protection. The cattle were herded into the lowest storey. Above it was the hall complete with fireplace and reached by a spiral staircase. Higher still was a kind of chamber for the women, and the flat roof was an admirable station from which the men could defend themselves.

In a commanding position, Dacre Castle is now a rather splendid private house. The moat is filled in, flowers and shrubs soften the aspect of the 8 ft. thick defensive walls, and a peacock struts the lawn with resplendent tail and strident voice. Across the meadow in the churchyard stand four massive chunks of stone in the form of bears. Weathered and worn, their features are no longer easy to discern. Their story is lost in time. Possibly they marked the four corners of a courtyard at the Castle. It is also believed this quiet village was the location of a monastery, and that the present church was preceded by a Saxon place of worship.

Also near Pooley Bridge is Eusemere where, in April 1802, William and Dorothy stayed with the Clarksons. Thomas Clarkson, one of the first men to concern himself with moves to abolish the slave trade, welcomed all the Wordsworth coterie to his home at differing times. As it turned out, no visit was to be more celebrated than this one. Walking through Gowbarrow Park the poet and his sister wandered into the wood towards Lyulph's Tower to see the first of the wild daffodils and then 'more and more'. Dorothy continues in her poetic prose—

> *'I never saw daffodils so beautiful, some rested their heads upon these stones as on a pillow for weariness, and the rest tossed and reeled and danced and seemed as if they verily laughed with the wind; they looked so gay, ever glancing, ever changing.'*

And the wind which tossed the daffodils, so unexpectedly discovered, swept across the lake—

> *'The bays were stormy and we heard the waves at different distances, and in the middle of the water like the sea.'*

Turning back they had to face the storm. The ferocity of the wind was such that even this stalwart pair, whom the weather rarely kept indoors, were thankful to be safely back at the Clarksons, and for the warm rum and water which awaited them. Next morning, true to the constantly changing mood of Lakeland weather, the storm was past, the hills were looking 'chearful' (sic) once again. Setting off early they walked to Brotherswater, over the Kirkstone and home to Rydal. Just an ordinary expedition which they took in their natural stride. Two years were to pass before William gave to the world the lines inspired by his memory of the wild daffodils, 'I wandered lonely as a cloud ...'.

Ullswater, regarded by some as the most beautiful lake of all, breaks away from the typical finger shape of the other lakes and curves into three separate reaches. Though apparently the first cartographers, taking little heed of this variation, caused Gray to remark, 'The figure of Ullswater nothing resembles that laid down in our maps'. From Pooley Bridge, where the River Eamont meanders out to the sea, and the hill of Dunmallet holds evidence of an ancient British fort, the prospect of the lowest reach is placid and serene. The gardens touching the river bank, and the somewhat urban aspect of the houses composing the end-of-lake village, remind us we are nearing the perimeter of the Lake District. Leaving the meadows of Watermillock and the low-lying fells to travel up beyond Skeely Nab and Hallin Fell, the mountains rise higher, growing in splendour as the longest and middle reach elbows round to Silver Point. Now the landscape of the flatter western shore displays the variegated woodland of the Gowbarrow and Glencoyne estates. Finally, forced to sweep round the imposing slopes of Place Fell, the lake changes course. Scattered towards the head are its handful of islets, House Holm off Silver Point, Lingy Holm opposite Mossdale Bay. Wall Holm is near Purse Point, and Cherry Holm the one we see from Glenridding. The change in direction evokes a heightening of anticipation, as the third reach moves between the parkland of Glencoyne and the indomitable Place Fell. Finally, at the lakehead, St. Sunday Crag and the group of peaks ruled over by Helvellyn create a climax little short of sublime.

In length, Ullswater is only exceeded by Windermere. Previously, before the tidy emergence of Cumbria, the county boundary went down the middle of the lake: the eastern shore paid allegiance to Westmorland, the west, north of Glencoyne Bridge, to Cumberland. Yet diversion has not entirely vanished. Various owners share the lake bed, the Lake District Special Planning Board and the Hassells of Dalemain having the larger portion. So although much of the shore is free to us

153

St. Patrick's Bay, Glenridding, Ullswater

all, visitors are advised to make local enquiries at the St. Patrick's boat landing concerning launching and mooring.

Although Derwentwater certainly gave sanctuary to St. Herbert, there is no evidence of any direct connection between the good St. Patrick and Ullswater, despite the church, the well, and, consequently, the boat landing, perpetuating his name. The most feasible explanation is that Patterdale, derived from *Patrichesdale*, was named after an early settler, Patrick, which suggested the dedication of the church to St. Patrick. It being generally accepted that many of the Norse settlers were from Ireland, the unknown Patrick, who colonised the narrow dale above Ullswater, was probably of Irish-Norse stock. Similarly, we may imagine a Norseman named Ulf, who, presumably, once owned Ullswater.

The lake of Ullswater, has, up to now, been deemed expansive enough to offer sport to both those whose idea of happiness is a quiet morning spent spinning for trout off Aira Point, and those to whom the lake is a superlative sheet of water on which to practise their ski-ing skill. The skiers have their club, and their own section of the foreshore at Howtown Bay, where, incidentally, there is the only public launching site for power-driven craft. Naturally, there is access for all types of

154

craft through some of the lakeshore camp sites, and Ulls-water has its own Yacht Club, its racing events and its August regatta.

The Lake Warden patrols the lake, as on Windermere, and skiers must abide by the Collision Rules. They must also re-frain from encroaching within the 10 mph speed limit operat-ing between Glenridding and Silver Point at the head, and from Pooley Bridge to Thwaitehill Neb at the foot. Before these restrictions came into force altercations between fisher-men and skiers were not unknown. It is impossible to please everybody. One of the conclusions of the Sandford Commit-tee was that 'noisy pursuits will nearly always be out of place in national parks'. In sympathy with this view, a recent further announcement by the Special Planning Board proposes that ski-ing on Ullswater should be gradually phased out. Natu-rally, there will be fervent opposition from the water skiers, and the outcome remains to be seen.

So at the present time, it is in the areas of restricted speed that the angler is more likely to be found fishing in peace beneath his green umbrella. Perch and trout are abundant, there are also skelly, once netted in their hundreds near Skelly Nab. But Ullswater has no pike, and the char became extinct probably due to some form of poisoning from the Greenside lead mine.

It has always seemed to me that the number of swan and duck on Ullswater is curiously small. But one of the winter sights is the gulls. Gulls fly inland to most of the lakes, but so many frequent Ullswater that their roost has been known to extend down the middle of the lake for about a mile.

Inevitably, Ullswater has not been immune from the con-flicting demands upon the lakes for recreation and economic use. Near Howtown is a plaque in memory of Lord Birkett, who was born in Ulverston and whose impassioned speech in the House of Lords saved Ullswater from being converted into a second Thirlmere. Nevertheless, the need for water re-mained. Manchester, temporarily thwarted in her quest, was determined to effect a solution. This time the Waterworks and the National Park followed a policy of close co-operation and extremely careful planning. Through their combined efforts and the advance of modern engineering, Manchester, unsuspected by us, does now pump away a percentage of water from the lake.

Near Pooley Bridge, a pumping station, located entirely below ground, has been in operation since 1972. After completion the whole site was landscaped into the surrounding contours, and after only a year or so the fields above had returned to grazing. The intake on the lake bed, about 60 ft. from the shore, is designed with a fixed weir so that the water will not leave the lake when it is below a prescribed level. This has ensured that, both in Ullswater and Windermere, where a similar scheme is operating, the city has its extra quota of water without affecting the life and natural beauty of either lake.

With the motorway only four miles to the east, Ullswater is within easy access of countless carloads of holidaymakers. For most of the season the beach at Glenridding is a hive of activity. Pupils setting off from the adjacent sailing school, visitors hiring row-boats, or starting up their outboard motors, are joined by others embarking on the passenger launch, *Raven*, for a leisurely cruise, or bound for the lonely fells above Howtown.

Howtown, beside a deep bay of the eastern shore, is a tiny place where much happens. From Glenridding it is reached by boat, or on foot, a superb walk around Place Fell. Apart from being the gateway to Martindale, Howtown harbours an Outdoor Activities Centre, a Mountain Rescue Team and the

The Raven approaching Howtown

Water Ski-ing Club. Not far away is Martindale church, which situated some 1,000 ft. or so above sea level is, in contrast to the liveliness of the lakeside, one of the most isolated places of worship in the country. And up on the fells three hundred red deer roam the only deer forest left in England. During the Middle Ages a party of their ancestors strayed from the Royal Forests of the Eden Valley, and made their way to these remote hills. Ever since they have been preserved, quite unenclosed, by the Hassell family.

Of course, road access to Howtown is by the shore from Pooley Bridge. Incidentally, this road was one of the first to see the newly innovated Royal Mail buses. Using a minibus instead of the familiar red van, the G.P.O. has thus given to a few pillar boxes a welcome secondary duty as bus stops. The road, frequented by a great many cars in summer, bravely divides into three ways, ending each time at Boredale, Bannerdale Head and Sandwick. After that it is walkers only. There are no other roads for miles around.

As the road comes to a full stop, so too does this brief tour draw to a close. We have travelled mostly by road. After all, if time is limited, it is the quickest means of journeying from lake to lake. But as we speed along the over-used tarmac, so much may be missed along the way. Because we have stayed in the valleys, 'beside the lake, beneath the trees', we have visited the popular spots, venturing but here and there on less peopled tracks. Certainly, these are harder to find than in the pre-car era, but it is still not necessary to climb the highest peaks to discover them. This land of lake and mountain has always been the walker's paradise. The walker is free to set of for as short, or as long a distance as legs and inclination dictate, whether it be over the fells, treading the lakeside paths, or even a few yards up a newly met byway. More will be seen, more will be heard, and the enduring appeal of this wild beauty will be known and understood. Only by abandoning the highways can you discover all the treasures of this part of our heritage which, with pride, will always be called the Lake District.

BIBLIOGRAPHY

Bate, Walter Jackson: *Coleridge* Weidenfeld & Nicolson 1969

Collingwood, W.G.: *Lake District History* Titus Wilson 1928

De Quincey, Thomas: *Recollections of the Lakes & the Lake Poets* Penguin 1970

Fraser, Maxwell: *Companion into Lakeland* Spurbooks 1970

Heaton Cooper, A.: *The English Lakes* Black 1905

Hervey, G.A.K. and Barnes, J.A.G.: *Natural History of the Lake District* Warne & Co. 1970

Knowles, Arthur: *With Campbell at Coniston* W. Kimber 1967

Lane, Margaret: *The Tale of Beatrix Potter* Warne & Co. 1968

Macan, T.T.: *Biological Studies of the English Lakes* Longman 1970

Macan, T.T. & Worthington, E.B.: *Life in Lakes & Rivers* Collins 1968

Millward, Roy, & Adrian Robinson: *The Lake District* Eyre & Spottiswode 1970

Rollinson, William: *A History of Man in the Lake District* Dent 1967

Ruskin, John: *Iteriad* F. Graham 1969

Sandilands, G.S.: *The Lakes* Muller 1947

Wheatley, Vera: *Life and Work of Harriet Martineau* Secker & Warburg 1957

Wordsworth, Dorothy: *Journals of Dorothy Wordsworth* Oxford 1971

Wordsworth, William: *Guide to the Lakes* O.U.P. 1970

INDEX

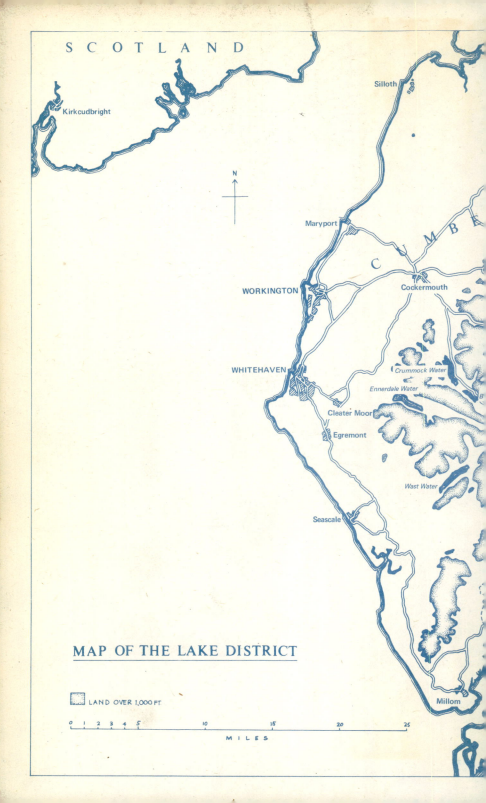

S C O T L A N D

Kirkcudbright

Silloth

N

Maryport

C U M B E

WORKINGTON

Cockermouth

WHITEHAVEN

Crummock Water

Ennerdale Water

Cleater Moor

Egremont

Wast Water

Seascale

MAP OF THE LAKE DISTRICT

LAND OVER 1,000 FT.

Millom

0 1 2 3 4 5   10   15   20   25

M I L E S